SANE RELATIONSHIPS

The Twelve Key Ideas That Make Sense of Relationships

By

Dr. Norman R. Wise

Sane Relationships:

The twelve key ideas that make sense of relationships

To Jon and Debbie Cooper

Introduction

Then the LORD God said, "It is not good that the man should be alone...."
(Genesis 2:18)

Human beings are social in nature. When we want to be very harsh to someone in prison we put them in solitary confinement.   They have the same food they had before and the same water. Yet, the very act of being isolated from all other human contact has been found to cause great pain psychologically in prisoners.   The depression that this environment encourages is so great that this is seen as one of the cruelest types of punishment possible.

The vast majority of human beings feel "pain" being cut off from human relationships. We experience loneliness which is a hunger and thirst of the soul for friendships. This inner drive causes us to seek others as friends, lovers, partners, and spouses. Few of us want to be alone, abandoned, and rejected by all other human beings. If we do then this normally means that we are struggling with some type of emotional or mental wound or illness.

Yet, even with all of this desire to connect and relate to others it is hard for human beings to relate to each other in healthy ways that lead to wholesome, encouraging, edifying, strengthening, and loving fellowship with each other.   We find ourselves experiencing some of the greatest pain of our lives due to involving ourselves with others. We suffer abuse, abandonment, rejection, and betrayal.   These experiences make us insecure in our relationships leading to jealousy, defensiveness, and fear. We find ourselves caught between the fear of being alone and the fear of being hurt by those we seek to love.

In addition, we find that at times we are triggered by other people so that we say and do things which reflect our darker and meaner side. When we are honest, we have to admit that we have hurt others, told lies, cheated, and failed to keep our promises.   We have not only suffered abuse but we have been the abuser of others.   Much of the shame and guilt we carry with us is because we know that we have not always treated other people well.

What was behind this manifestation of evil actions and words?   If we reflect, many of us can see that we have desired to have power and control over others so that we could feel safer and more secure.   To gain this power and control we would many times hurt those we said we loved.   Abuse gave us control over others and control over others gave us security and fed our pride.

It is hard to make sense of relationships. Most of us experience our most crazy moments due to the dynamics of attempting to work with, love, and be with other people.   It is very hard to do relationships well.

What are we attempting to gain in our relationships?   There are basically five positive realities we hope to experience by relating to others.

1.   Life - We know that we are safer when we are surrounded by family and friends. Our ability to survive and thrive is greater with a network of people who are our allies and associates.   It is safer in the "jungle" of life if one belongs to a "village" of people who will be there to help in times of crisis, sickness, and threat.

2. Love – We all want to love and be loved.   Our relationships allow us to express all the different types of love we have within us. We can give and receive love in mentoring, parenting, friendships, partnerships, romances, and marriages.   In the mix of these relationships we feel that we are valued and recognize the value of others.   Our sense of giving to others through our love helps our self image and appreciation for what others give to us provides for us joy and security.

3.   Learning – While we may learn some by independent research of the physical world or out of private musings; in reality all of our learning takes place by standing on the shoulder of giants. We learn our first words from those around us and the significant adults in our lives, mentor us for good or evil from our earliest days.

Normally we have a bond of affection, appreciation, loyalty and debt to those who have taught, coached, challenged, dialoged, and shared with us their training, thoughts, and truth.   Those who have been our teachers, coaches, and mentors both formally and informally have normally felt a bond of affection, care, and devotion to us as well. Eventually, we will become the teacher, coach, and mentor to others and will also know the affection the sage has for the student.

4. Laughter – It is possible for us to laugh alone but normally only when it is stimulated by some thought of other people. Our best laughter comes when we share it in joyful and fun times together with others. There is a human bond formed by sharing times of entertainment, excitement, games, fun, recreation and eating together. There is a special bond that takes place when people have a party together and celebrate in oneness of heart.

5. Legacy – There is a deep desire for us to leave to others good after we die. We want people to relate to us after we die with love, honor, and respect. There is a desire to relate to future generations with a positive impact of service and giving. We want to imagine people speaking at our funeral remembering us with love and respect as the recount that our lives were lived with virtue and wisdom.

These five core human needs of life, love, learning, laughter, and legacy all have aspects of them that can only be experienced by healthy human relationships. If we fail at relationships then our life, love, learning, laughter, and legacy will be diminished. So knowing how to wisely invest and succeed in relationships is a vital skill to learn. We want to know how to have sane and stable interactions with other people. This is a vital life skill.

Most people just "do" relationships and have not studied relationships. They have approached the relationships of life from the perspective of "Ready, Fire, Aim" instead of "Ready, Aim, Fire". The results have for the most part been disastrous.

Relationships like every other aspect of life are governed by certain "laws" or "principles" which if mastered help us be successful and if violated will bring failure. This book will hope to outline and make practical the 12 key ideas that govern effective relationships so that everyone can master them and so improve their life, love, learning, laughter, and legacy. There is no reason to think that relationships are ruled by chaos instead of logic. We can have sane relationships and make sense of them.

Now what would it mean to succeed at relationships? Success is when I treat any subject in a sane, stable, and spiritual manner. The only control I have in my life or in any relationship is over myself. I can choose to be sane, stable, and spiritual in how I deal with other people. This is the one and only thing I control in the relationship.

The goal then is to define what is sane, stable, and spiritual to do moment by moment in a relationship and to do it. We get "Ready and Aim" by defining and planning exactly what being sane, stable, and spiritual is; in every circumstance with each individual person. If we can understand this then the directing of our energy into productive words, actions, and attitudes is much more likely.

Now we will be recommending that we learn to respond instead of react. Reactive relationships go off like fire crackers whose fuses have been lit. They have no more thought in them than a knee jerk responding to a doctor's hammer during a physical exam. Our words, actions, and attitudes just pour out of us reacting to whatever the other person did, said, or implied.

Responsive relationships are where we never react but always carefully, thoughtfully, and prayerfully choose every word, deed, and attitude. Our aim is to do what is responsible in the circumstances regardless if the other person has acted in a responsible manner. To be responsible is to be "response able" or able to give a sane, stable, and spiritual reply to each person in each relationship. We will think before we speak or act. This is the only sane way to live.

The chapters in this book will focus on looking at twelve key beliefs that will control how well we relate to others. You will be challenged to define the problem you are having in each of these key areas of belief and how you could plan to improve it. Each chapter will end with a group of reflective questions that will challenge you to use what you have read.

This book is only successfully read if you use it to actually change and improve your thinking and doing. So, I ask you to plan right now not just to "read" this book but instead to "apply" this book into your life. If you do this then the time you take reading the book cannot be wasted but simply a wise investment in finding how to have sane relationships with other people.

Reflective Questions

1. List all the key relationships in your life. Separate them into two groups.

The first group mark of as your "inner circle" who you share your thoughts, feelings, and who you are with. You would say these people know you and you know them. These people would be with you during your most difficult times and give you "the shirt of their backs" if they needed to in order to help.

Then put the rest of the people in your life in a group which we will call "my village". These are people that know about you and you would not mind going to a party with them. These people would be there to help you in an emergency as long as it did not require a huge sacrifice.

2. List your satisfaction with your current experience of:

Life

Love

Learning

Laughing

Legacy

On a scale form 1-10 with 1 being almost no satisfaction to 10 being perfect satisfaction.   What could you do to improve your satisfaction in any of these five areas?

3. Do you know of any emotional trigger in your life that causes you to "react" with negative words, actions, and attitudes? What is it? How could you gain self control over this area so that it does not so easily set you off?

Chapter One: The Foundation of Good Relationships

Know yourself – Socrates

The unexamined life is never lived well – paraphrased Socrates

Strangely enough to have a good relationship with others we must first have a good relationship with ourselves. Many people who do not like themselves are hoping that other people will like them. Some of us are even hoping to learn to accept ourselves because others accept us.

So the first relationship that we must make healthy and upon which all other relationships will be healthy is with ourselves. If we do not love ourselves in a proper and healthy way then we will not be able to love others in a proper and healthy way. A strong relationship with others begins by us having a solid foundation of understanding ourselves that is honest, real, and compassionate.

Who are you?

So who are you? That is an important question for you to answer. To know yourself you need to take an inventory of your experience up to this present time. You need to sort through the significant moments in your life and divide them into four categories.

1. Circumstances, events, and people who caused me pain and harm.

2. Words, actions, and attitudes in which I caused other people pain and harm. This should be broken up into two groups. One group is where I did not intend harm to others and the other is where I did intend harm to others.

3. Circumstances, events and people who caused me pleasure, helped me reach a goal, encouraged me, and provided me real help in life.

4. Words, actions, and attitudes in which I caused people pleasure and gave them help. This could be broken up into two groups. One group is where I did not intend to help others but did and the other is where I did intend to help.

The following chart may help you sort this out.

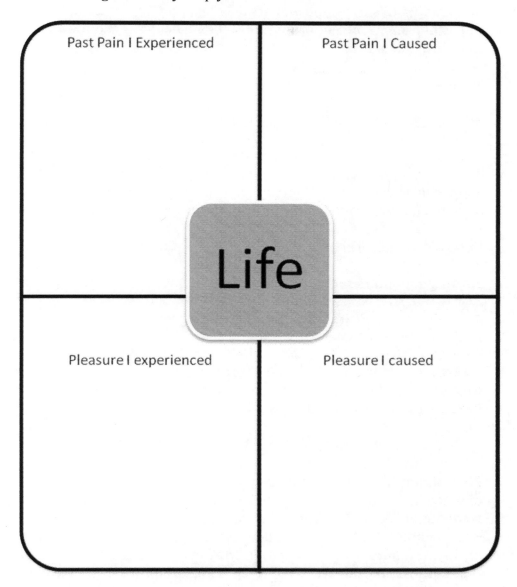

Now what I would like you to do right now is just stop reading and spend one hour working on listing the key events that fit each category. I would like you to spend fifteen minutes on each area. That would mean spend fifteen minutes listing and thinking about the pain others have caused you, fifteen minutes listing times when you hurt others, fifteen minutes remembering how others have helped you, and finally fifteen minutes making an inventory of how you have been a source of blessing to other people.

By spending this hour you will actually be applying what this chapter is teaching about the importance of self knowledge. To know yourself you must take time with yourself. You must also bring to your conscious mind the reality of who you are and what you have experienced.

HOW DO YOU FEEL ABOUT YOUR LIFE?

How do you feel about your life and what you have experienced? It is important to know how we have emotionally responded to what has happened to us. Our emotional state largely reflects how we have responded to what has occurred up to this time in our lives.

So how do you feel about:

1. The painful times in your life
2. The times you caused pain to others
3. The times when others focused on helping you
4. The times when you were a blessing to other people

Sometimes we lack words to express our emotions. Here is a list of words that will help you describe in greater detail and accuracy how you feel about each aspect of your life.

Emotional List of Words

Pain, frustration, fear, panic, confusion, anger, hatred, disgust, sick, disoriented, surprise, curious, pleasure, happy, joy, peace, contentment, desire, passionate, lustful, bored, exited, proud, humble, guilt, shame, crazy, desperate, depressed, sad, despair, focused, blind, brilliant, dumb, overwhelmed, competent, lost, thankful, hunger, thirst, satisfied, embarrassed, love, compassion, caring, concerned, worried, anxious, centered, scattered, secure, prayerful, accepted, abandoned, rejected, desired, trustful, doubting

So now summarize the key emotions listed with each area. What emotions were created by the times of pain, our moral failures, the times of pleasure, and the times of service? Sort out your emotions for each of these times in your life. Which of these emotions are the strongest in you today? Which are the weakest? How much do these emotions impact your day by day life?

Your current emotional state is the sum of all of these emotions and the degree you have successfully processed them.

WHAT TO YOU THINK ABOUT YOUR LIFE?

Now that you have put together this summary of key events and people in your life; you can now analyze your life. Out of these events what wisdom have you developed? What proverbs and life rules would you pass on to others based on your experience? What ideas now control your words, actions, and attitudes? Where did these ideas come from?

Answer the following question; what have I learned about life?

Summary of my "Life Wisdom"

Imagine that your life has been written into a book. What section in the book store do you feel would best describe your life up to the present time? If you were to think of your life as a story would it be a comedy, a drama, a tragedy, fiction, self help, religious, soup for the soul, horror, or a mystery. Maybe none of these describe it. How would you describe it? Write out your description here.

Who am I?

Up to this point we have come to know how the things that have happened to us and the things we have done have formed to create our lives. But there is more to us than just our environment and past experiences. There is a core of our personalities that needs to be understood. We also need to understand this if we are to effectively relate to others.

There are four basic personalities types that I believe have been created by God. Each personality type is needed and is "good" within the framework of how it can be used. At the same time each personality type also faces some specific temptations and struggles. Understanding our basic personality type if important when we relate to others. It is also important to remember that not everyone has the same personality type.

These four personality types are:

The Leader
The Networker
The Organizer
The Healer

What are the characteristics of these four types? How do they differ" Which one am I?

The Leader

There is much debate about if leadership can be taught. Regardless if it can be taught or not there are some people who simply have the "gift" or ability to lead which seems to be a part of the core make up of their being. They do not have to be trained or taught how to lead they just do lead and people follow. They have "charisma" that allows people to believe what they say and trust their direction. They were born to lead.

We need not look very far to find a leadership personality in our family, business, church, or community. They are the ones that are always "looking for a superior method" or building a "better mouse trap". They have an entrepreneurial streak and don't mind taking risk in order to receive the rewards that can go along with it. They are people of vision, passion, and energy. They know where they are going and easily invite others to join them as allies on their great quest. They get joy from reaching self defined goals.

The leadership personality is usually very self-governing, undeviating and to the point. They will probably tell you to "get to the bottom line" or give them the "executive summary" to examine. They don't like everyday processes and often delegate routine daily tasks to someone else.

The leadership personality enjoys change, and one of their biggest fears is falling into a "rut". They are very alert on what they are doing and are normally not sensitive to others that might be around them. If they tell somebody something, or explain it, they'll say it ONCE and expect that every person in the group is listening and has understood. They are ready to keep moving towards the goal.

Do you have some degree of leadership in your personality? Do you know someone who is naturally a leader? Would you feel comfortable seeing yourself as a leader?

Now under this general leadership personality there are four different types of leadership personality.

1. Supervisor – These leaders are hard working, logical, responsible, and care about facts not theories or feelings. They want to make sure that everything runs effectively and systematically in their lives and whatever organization they find themselves involved in. They like to build upon traditions and want everyone to follow clear standards of behavior and beliefs.

2. Persuader – Follows the approach of "Ready, Fire, Aim". They love action over planning. They have strong "charisma" and people like them. They can think on their feet and change direction quickly. They want quick results and can solve problems on the run. They handle criticism well, are filled with enthusiasm, and are very excited about reaching their goals. They look to the present circumstances, quickly decide what should be done, see to it that it is done, and are ready for the next challenge.

3. Captain – These leaders are long term plans and believe in having things well organized. They know how to coordinate people in complex organizational structures and come up with intelligent solutions. They believe in "Ready, Aim, Fire". They like knowing the facts, being efficient, and doing things right the first time. They love to lead, overcome challenges, see new possibilities, and have the ability to quickly understand complex situations and find a solution to bring about success.

4. The Mastermind – They see the world as a giant chess board and are always seeing strategic plans that will have high payoffs. They are also aware of alternative plans should things happen they do not foresee. These people don't like to talk about feelings, are very analytical, and calculating. They lead through intellectual power and vision.

People who follow may not like them but they are respected. They are "system builders" and will do anything to reach their goals. They are obsessed by winning. They are quiet leaders who are very objective, adaptable, and unemotional. They are supreme planners who are always striving to get new ideas and concepts that may improve their current approach to be adopted.

Do any of these descriptions fit you? Do you think you may be a combination of a couple of the different descriptions found here?

Do you know people that fit these types? Try to list one person you know by each type of leader. Which type of leader do you follow best? Which type of leader do you think is best? Does this help you understand this yourself a little better?

The Networker

If you are a "Networker" personality type, you are concerned about communication and people. Networkers are optimistic, appealing, and outgoing. They are a "people persons." This type of person genuinely is fond of people, and wants to be liked. Networkers trust people and enjoy bringing out their best. People with this personality are expert communicators.

A Networker enjoys telling stories and tends to exaggerate. They enjoy meeting new people, working with others, and networking. A networker tends to ignore the rules since they stand in the way of relating to people personally.

Networkers are cheerleaders for the ideas of leaders and provide a social catalyst critical to getting people to work together. They follow the leader because they "like" the leader more than they like the ideas of the leader. For a networker everything is personal.

Networkers are animated by working with people and energize any group they work with.   A person who is a networker sees the "big picture" presented by the leader and can be motivating.   Normally most networkers have a dislike for details and can lack focus on goals since people are more important.

Networkers do not want the responsibility of leadership. They like to work in groups and feel a part of them. A networker enjoys the relationships in the group more than reaching a particular goal. They can reach goals but not at the expense of people. People are their world.

Are you a networking personality? Do you connect with people naturally and help groups connect? Do you know someone like that?

Now under the network personality there are four different types of network personalizes.

Nurturer – These people love to honor and celebrate traditional holidays, emotionally important days, and birthdays. They want everyone in an organization or family to work together without conflict. They will organize special events with the focus on people relating to people during these special times. They have the ability to bring out the best in others. They will get things done effectively in order to bring about a social event. They are warm and caring. They seek to meet the needs of people in a very practical manner. They aim at developing and encouraging people.

Entertainer – These people love to be with people and hate to be alone. They focus on being the center of attention and getting everyone laughing or in a good mood. Entertainers like action and animation. They are able to bond people together. They will harness the energy of the people in an organization to take on exciting challenges that the leader has chosen. Entertainers accept and relate with people as they are without judgment. They are able to understand what is essential in order to motivate other people to get jobs done. They prefer a work setting that is energetic, action oriented, and without disagreement.

Instigator – These people are usually verbally quick and will interrupt others to get their thoughts out. They are mentally inventive and put things together in new ways. They love to debate, discuss, and dialogue about ideas in a group. They look at an "argument" as a type of sport and are not easily offended. Instigators are thick skinned and may appear rude to people at times. Yet, their positive nature and persistence actually attract people. They want to change the way people think and encourage people to try new things. They like to start things but don't like to get stuck in something for a long time simply maintaining things. They like fresh relationships and projects over what has become routine.

True Believers – These people are affectionate, passionate people, typically with high IQs and jam-packed with potential. They want to create a community that will change the world for the better. Following a visionary leader they will organize people together into a fellowship of "true believers" which will be filled with love, harmony, and peace. They live in the universe of possibilities, and can become very fervent and energized about fixing social systems that will help people. Their passion and optimism enables to unite, inspire and motivate other people. They can talk their way in or out of anything. They enjoy being alive and strive to make everyone see how wonderful life can be.

Do any of these descriptions fit you? Do you think you may be a combination of a couple of the different descriptions found here? Do you know people that fit these types? Try to list one person you know by each type of leader. Does this help you understand who you are?

The Organizer

Organizers like to adhere to rules, regulations, logical systems, and organization. They like to do high quality work, in an ethical manner, in a systematic manner, and do it right the first time. These people are careful, cautious, exacting, neat, systematic, accurate, and thoughtful. These people make great scientists, engineers, and accountants. They are very detailed focused.

Organizers are more concerned about procedures than people. They will challenge leaders if they believe that pragmatism is winning over principles. They disagree with ever taking a short cut to get things done. What is important is that it is done right. They can be tempted to be judgmental and critical when people do not meet their expectations and standards of performance.

Do you have some degree of being an organizer in your personality? Do you know someone who is naturally an organizer? Would you feel comfortable seeing yourself as an organizer?

Now under this general organizer personality there are four different styles of organizer personality.

Examiners – These people are very faithful, realistic, and dependable. Examiners place great significance on honesty and integrity. They focus on being "good people" who can be trusted to do the moral thing for their families and communities. They are hard workers and create systems to guarantee quality work.

Examiners are very aware of time and will always be punctual. They have a great concern about wasting time. They are "super dependable" and set high standards of performance and character for themselves and everyone else. They will find mistakes and address them to leadership.

Mechanic – These people can take anything mechanical apart and put it back together. They can be either men or women. Mechanics like to work with their hands and by themselves. They can find ways to "fix things" in a realistic and logical way. They can see the easiest and most practical route to completing a task, and they hate to waste their efforts on unnecessary things.

Mechanics often act as trouble shooters, rising to meet the needs of an emergency situation when things break. Mechanics know lots of technical information in their area of interest and passion. They are great resource people filled with "how to" information that can be vital to a group.

Artist - These people live in the world of taste, smell, looks, sound, and touch. They are very physical people and normally love nature. They have a strong aesthetic appreciation for art, and are likely to be artists in some form, because they are unusually gifted at creating and composing things which will strongly impact the senses.

They want things to look right, smell right, feel right, sound right and taste right. They hate the ugly, unclean, or disorganized. Beauty, harmony, and physical order are more important than people. They are attracted to what is physically beautiful. They know how to be very exact and precise in creating or appreciating music, food, or art.

Engineer - These people live in their own logical minds. Extremely strong in math they see everything in terms of an equation. They are normally quiet and easy going except when one of their key principles or "equations" is violated. They hate anything that is illogical and can express great anger and outrage at what they see at violating their inner "logic". They hate things not to "add up".

Uneasy with conflict these explosions will normally not last long and they prefer to return to their inner worlds since they are easily embarrassed if they become the center of attention. For an engineer every incident is to be rigorously dissected by logic and reason. The focus of the engineers mind is to fit very experience of life into a larger structure defined by logic."

Do any of these descriptions fit you? Do you think you may be a combination of a couple of the different descriptions found here? Do you know people that fit these types? Try to list one person you know by each styles of organizer. Does this help you yourself?

The Healer

Healers are focused on helping, caring, teaching, and nurturing. They are normally "slow and steady" and hate to be hurried or overwhelmed with work. They are normally seen as stable people and are those that people depend on during hard times. Healers live to support and to serve other people.

Healers are trustworthy and reliable; however they need to be given assurance that their relationships are secure. These people will help to create a peaceful environment and will avoid destructive conflict at all costs. They are natural peacemakers. Healers are reliable and hard working, however, they don't work well under pressure and they don't like deadlines.

People with this personality need lots of supervision by leaders. They will get so involved in helping people that they will forget organizational goals. Healers work well within a tightly knit team and love to feel like part of a small group aimed at healing others. If they disagree with a leader they won't normally speak up but instead will attempt to work behind the scenes to get things to change or get other people to openly confront the leader.

Healers need written directions to refer back to and require assistance when starting new projects. People with this personality will prefer small groups of friends and consistent familiar environments over large events and meeting new people. Healers are self controlled and modest. They will ask people who work for them to do things rather than tell them to do something. Many times they will just do things themselves rather than risk a conflict.

Healers make great counselors, teachers, and social workers. They are the compassionate glue that keeps organizations together. Healers give heart, warmth, compassion, and social vision to every family or group.

Do you have some degree of being a healer in your personality? Do you know someone who is naturally a healer? Would you feel comfortable seeing yourself as a healer?

Now under this general healer personality there are four different styles of healer personality.

Guardian - The primary desire of the guardian is to serve others by keeping people safe and secure. They need to be needed in relationships. Guardians are loyal, sympathetic, consistent, and considerate in their service to others. They are known for their compassion, sympathy, gentleness and for their willingness to go to any length to help those in need.

Guardians focus on the practical needs of people when they do their work, and their strong focus on details allows them to carry out organizational goals. They will do more than expected of them, without attracting attention to themselves. They are careful and accountable with detail and routine that is aimed at helping people, and feel it is important to have the right things in the right places at the right times so that the needs of people are met.

2. Mentor – These people are very introspective, caring, and people centered. They have a desire to be supportive, encouraging, and act as a coach in people's lives. They attract people to their cause by their warmth of character and desire to build a better world. They are easily hurt and do not handle critical remarks well. Their greatest desire is to leave behind a legacy that has helped people in concrete ways. Mentors hope to leave a group of transformed lives which will in turn transform other lives.

3. Counselor – These people have a great clarity about the inner world of the emotions and mind. They seem to intuitively understand others. Other people trust them. There is a feeling of sanity, stability, and spirituality that is felt in their presence by others. They appear to others to have it "together".

Counselors desire to contribute to the welfare of others and genuinely enjoy helping the "souls" of others. These people tend to be private and sensitive people. Counselors will exert their influence behind the scenes by giving advice to people one on one. Others naturally seek out people with this personality when they want to gain inner clarity and peace of mind.

4. Idealists – These people have great faith in great principles that will selflessly live and die for what they consider to be true. They hunger to know and understand the meaning and value of life. Idealists want to know the truth and live the truth because they believe this will bring the greatest blessing to the most people.

Their idealism is always connected to their caring for people. They serve people by serving the truth. They promote faith, hope, and love in families and communities.

Do any of these descriptions fit you? Do you think you may be a combination of a couple of the different descriptions found here? Do you know people that fit these types? Try to list one person you know by each type of healer. Does this help you understand this yourself?

Take some time right now to review this last section. Write out a description of who you are based on this discussion. You cannot have sane relationships with others unless you have carefully and prayerfully thought about who you are and also about the basic personality types of the other key people in your life.

For additional reading on this topic I would recommend the following books.

1. *Knowing Me, Knowing God: Exploring Your Spirituality with Myers-Briggs*. Malcolm Goldsmith
2. *Gifts Differing: Understanding Personality Type* by Isabel Briggs Myers
3. *Understanding How Others Misunderstand You* by Ron Braund and Ken Voges

A study and reflection in which we define our core personality and know who we are is a vital step in being prepared to have sane relationships with others.

WHAT DOES THIS HAVE TO DO WITH RELATIONSHIPS?

Now what does all this have to do with relationships? Well this is the part of the "baggage" that you carry with you into every other relationship in your life. Some people know their baggage and are aware of how it can impact their reactions to things. They therefore can choose to take this into account and instead of react; they can choose a proper response.

Many people don't really know their baggage. They choose to deny it or suppress it. In their minds they are walking into every relationship like a clean slate and free of any past events. They want to ignore the impact that personality types have had on past relationships or how it is impacting the present group of relationships.

Now we can have other types of emotional baggage. This can be from the pain and pleasures we have experienced in life. These experiences can "color" and define how we see and hear others.

When we don't process our emotional "baggage" then it will influence us to "react" and release a ton of emotions into the present reality of life that mostly come from unresolved issues. We find ourselves not wanting to understand others but instead judging and condemning them. This flood of emotions rarely works in our favor and normally escalates a bad circumstance into a worst one.

We must recognize that we have a responsibility to process, heal from, learn, and develop from our experiences. Relationships with people must not become our way of healing our painful past. This will make the relationship "co-dependent" and this will put a strain on it that it cannot endure. If we bring to a relationship a soul that lacks sanity, stability, and spirituality, we can be assured that the relationship is not going to solve that problem.

We have all seen this in the "rebound relationship" cycle. Someone suffers the death of a relationship. This can be caused by a death, divorce, or separation. They feel abandoned, rejected, and question their worth. To deal with this pain they seek out a relationship with another person as quickly as possible to help them get over the relationship they lost.

These "rebound relationships" almost always lack sanity and stability. They do not really heal the hurt caused by the loss even if they temporary kill the pain. There is a difference between a cure and a pain killer. Here the heart needs to be healed before the person is ready to get into another relationship.

Also, if I don't recognize that I have a particular personality and other people have different personalities then I can have false expectations that everyone will approach life the same way. By recognizing my personality type I can better comprehend why others may struggle in understanding me if their personality type is different.

Also, every personality type can be expressed in a healthy or unhealthy manner. Knowing what the temptations of our particular personality type are can be helpful. The bottom line is this; to be effective in relationships with others we need to have a deep knowledge and acceptance of ourselves.

So one vital aspect of having a solid foundation for relationships is having a knowing who we are and what has influenced us. This knowledge will be vital if we are to be effective in sharing with others who we are. Without self knowledge then emotional intimacy is impossible.

How do I get to know myself?

Now relationships can help us in our understanding of ourselves. To understand this we need to understand that there are four aspects of self knowledge.

1. What I think I know about myself
2. What I share with other about myself
3. What others think they know about me that I do not know
4. What no one but God knows about who I am

Each of us has a "self perception". This is how we see ourselves in our minds. Some of this "self perception" can be very realistic and true. Some of it is an illusion and a lie. We can deny a weakness and exaggerate strength. It is also possible for us to ignore ability we do have and desire a talent we do not have.

I became aware of this in my perception of my singing abilities. I was in seventh grade and everyone had to be in the choir. I loved to sing. I sang at church, in the shower, and just walking down the street. I found comfort in singing. In my own view of myself I was a great singer. Because of this I sang boldly and loudly.

The music director at our school at the end of the semester was ending our time together by making a few fun comments to the class. He pointed me out and said I was a perfect example of a person who had great passion and no ability. He chuckled as he reflected on how "Norm sings like a wounded bandit. " I am sure that he thought I already knew this fact.

This was the first objective feedback I had been given on my singing. I suddenly recognized that other people were not hearing what I heard in my head. My perception was a false one. I was not a great singer. I still love to sing. I still find comfort in singing. I am just aware that I don't sing well and that it is not an enjoyable experience for others. So now I sing privately or softly. Sometimes I just let my "wounded bandit" loose but with no illusions about how it sounds to others.

This illustrates another reality. Sometimes people have knowledge of us that we lack. Because they can see our body language and have an objective perspective on our words and deeds they sometimes can see things we miss. By listening to the feedback from others on their perception of us we can grow in an accurate knowledge of ourselves. This can help us be more realistic about who we are at times.

Now the danger here is that others may have wrong perceptions about who we are. Their view of us may be influenced by their own "baggage" and they may be looking at us through "colored glasses". Some men see all women as untrustworthy and therefore interpret women through prejudiced eyes. There are women based on suffering abuse that see all men as dangerous. So we cannot just accept the feedback from others about who they see us to be as objective fact and truer than our self perception automatically.

Instead we have to weigh what they have said and see if we believe it to be valid or not. To never take feedback from others is to be guilty of pride and to always take their feedback is to be gullible. We have to filter the feedback carefully and decide if it is accurate or false. Now of course it could be partly true and partly inaccurate as well. We must decide how valid the feedback is. But getting defensive over all negative feedback will hurt every relationship in our lives.

Feedback by the way can be positive as well as negative. I did not see myself as a teacher. A senior in my college came to me my freshman year and took me aside. He said that he believed that I had a great potential for teaching people. Another senior gave me the opportunity to teach weekly in a high school group he ran. The students loved my teaching. This insight that I came to see was true has encouraged me to teach for over thirty years.

Now my knowledge of myself is all that I can choose to share with others.   To the degree I decide to share what I think, how I feel, and my perception of who I see myself; I have emotional intimacy with another person. Emotional intimacy is sharing my thoughts, feelings, and self image with another.

Now we are not at the same level of emotional intimacy with all people.   But it is important to know that emotional intimacy is and what has to be communicated to achieve it.

Conclusion

To make have sane relationships with others I have to have a sane understanding of myself.   I have to know my history, good and bad. I have to have a clear understanding of my personality.   I have to have insight into how I am different than the other key people in my life. I have to know how to grow in my own knowledge of myself by receiving the feedback of other people. By doing this I have laid an important foundation for being sane in how I relate to others.

Reflective Questions

1.   Summarize your life story in three paragraphs.   In the first paragraph describe where you have been in the past.   Next, in the second paragraph, describe where you are at the present moment. Dedicate the last paragraph to stating what you would like the future to look like.

2.   Write a one page description of your personality type.   Use whatever words or descriptions you feel will help you understand yourself.   What are the strengths of your personality?   What are the weaknesses?   How are the three most important people in your life similar or different from you in personality and how does this impact your relationships?

Chapter Three – Making Sense of the Most Important Relationship

THE MOST INTIMATE KNOWLEDGE OF WHO I AM COMES FROM GOD

"Our wisdom, in so far as it ought to be deemed true and solid Wisdom, consists almost entirely of two parts: the knowledge of God and of ourselves. But as these are connected together by many ties, it is not easy to determine which of the two precedes and gives birth to the other. For, in the first place, no man can survey himself without forthwith turning his thoughts towards the God in whom he lives and moves; because it is perfectly obvious, that the endowments which we possess cannot possibly be from ourselves; nay, that our very being is nothing else than subsistence in God alone." John Calvin

There is one relationship that is critical to every other relationship we have in our lives. That is the relationship we have with God. Now as you related events, circumstances, and people that caused you pain and pleasure you either included references to God, Christ, Spirit, and religious representatives as key events in your story or they were absent. Different people respond to the question of God in diverse ways. Yet, there is no doubt that this will impact how we interact with people and ourselves.

For those who say there is no God this also means that there are aspects of who we are that are unknown to everyone. No person knows them so there is a part of who we are that is shrouded in not being known at all. There can be hope that perhaps in dialogue or self examination one might learn a new aspect of who we are but it is very possible that some of who we are will remain unknown forever. The universe in this perspective is ultimately impersonal and who we are is ultimately unknown and unknowable.

For the one who believes in God there is the confidence that the creator of the universe and of my soul fully understands every aspects of who I am. Nothing about me is hidden from HIM. It is also possible that God might reveal to me that which is hidden from me so prayer for self revelation has hope of being answered. I do know that ultimately I am known by the one who is ultimate. There is one who has intimate knowledge of me and before whom nothing is hid or wrongly interpreted. This makes the universe ultimately personal.

Now which perspective is right? About 90% of Americans believe that the best understanding of reality is that God exists. I believe that this is the truth. I believe in a Christian world view and that includes faith in God being real.

Now for my friends who do not believe in God; I would challenge you to think about how your perception about God impacts how you see people? To what extent is your vision of the world as only materialistic or naturalistic; impact how you relate to others? Do you think it has any impact?

I would also recommend that you read How To Think About God by Mortimer Adler who was the head of the philosophy department at the University of Chicago and Does God Exist by Kai Nielsen and J.P. Moreland. These books point out that there are people who have carefully and rationally considered the issue of God's existence and trust in this existence due to what they believe to be sound reasons. So if you have never considered the reasons for belief in God that may be a worthwhile process to engage in.

Relationships Seek "Shalom" or Peace

Relationships are at the heart of how we see the world. The Hebrew concept of "Shalom" or PEACE is all based on relationships. This concept is helpful in creating a correct framework for understanding relationships.

To have "Shalom" is to have the right relationship with God, the right relationship with my soul, the right relationship with others, and the right relationship with impersonal circumstances. So to be sanity in relationships is learning how to be at peace and experience "Shalom" in all aspects of my life.

Shalom is having four relationships be right!

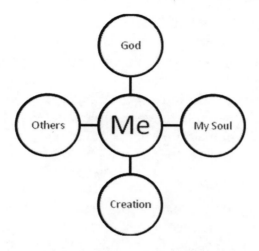

Finding Peace in My Relationship With God

Our human relationships are influenced by how content, peaceful, secure, hopeful, and forgiving we are. All of these can be influenced by having a right relationship with God. For many the foundation of how they relate to people is grounded in how they perceive their relationship with the Creator. Therefore, our spiritual vision can be a vital aspect of how well we treat others and are successful in our associations with other people.

So how can we be in right relationship with God? There are two theories about how this can be achieved. The one is represented in many formal religions but also in just what appears common sense to many people. The other one is based on the teachings and life of Jesus of Nazareth who is considered to be the promised Messiah of the Hebrew Bible. We will compare both of these approaches and evaluate which one can guide us in seeking a right relationship with God.

Theory One: I have a right relationship with God based on living right

The basic idea of this world view is that

- God created humanity
- Humanity has a moral responsibility before God
- Some human beings are responsible and good and others are not responsible and are evil
- God is in right relationship with those who are good
- At death God will judge people and will reward the good people and punish the evil people
- To have a right relationship with God I need to do more good than evil.

This is "theology 101". Most people who believe in God at some gut level hold to this perspective. The details can change because of tradition, religious philosophy, culture, and family traditions but at core this is the theory about God that people hold to and express when they talk about their relationship with God.

Now you have two different schools of thought within this theory. One is the "loose" school. From this perspective any person who is generally a "nice" person and avoids doing really major league "evil" things like mass murder, torture, or rape will accepted by God. God in this version grades on a curve and very few people "fail" the moral test that God gives at the end of life. This view is very optimistic about eternity and sees God as generally pleased with people since they are basically "good".

This is the theory most popular in the United States right now. According to the Gallup Poll:

"In 1988, Gallup asked Americans who said there is a heaven where people who had led good lives are eternally rewarded what their chances were of going there themselves. Seventy-seven percent rated their chances as "good" or "excellent," while 19% rated them as "only fair" or "poor." That same year, Americans who said there was a hell where people who led bad lives without being sorry are eternally damned were quite optimistic that they would not be going there themselves. Only 6% said their chances of going there were good or excellent, and 79% said their chances were poor." (http://www.gallup.com/poll/11770/eternal-destinations-americans-believe-heaven-hell.aspx)

So most Americans feel that they do have a right relationship with God because they see themselves as moral people who have led a sufficiently good life to earn eternal fellowship and reward with God. While this may not mean that they feel a close relationship with God on a daily basis; overall most Americans believe that God is on their side and happy with how they are living.

The second group within this theory holds to a "strict" perspective on morals. They believe that only by striving for true excellence in worship and service to others will a person earn a right relationship with God. They would believe that only a few actually attain this degree of moral excellence and so few people will actually attain "heaven" or a place of happy fellowship with God when they die. Few within this group would feel that they have attained the degree of moral excellence to be accepted God. Some in this group hold to a process after death that allows people to continue to strive to gain a right relationship with God. This group is far less optimistic about their relationship with God and experience some degree of anxiety over what will happen when they or loved ones die.

This is the first theory about how to have a right relationship with God. This theory is based on our performance and earning God's acceptance by doing good deeds and avoiding evil. This perspective is very popular both in the United States and in the world generally. It would seem to be the most basic approach that human beings have when thinking about God.

Theory Two: I have a right relationship with God based on God giving me a loving relationship as a free gift

The basic idea of this world view is that

There is Bad News

- God created humanity with a responsibility to love
- God is fully committed to love and being just
- A just God must judge people when they fail their responsibility to love
- God who is love is in right relationship with those who love perfectly as God loves perfectly
- All human beings have failed to love as they should love
- Every human being is living under God's condemnation and judgment because of failing to love as they should love

There is Good News

- God out of love decided to send the Messiah Jesus who was "God in the flesh" from heaven to earth to live the perfect life of love and then receive the punishment for our lack of love so that we could have a right relationship with God.

"For our sake God made Jesus the Messiah to be a payment for sin who knew no sin, so that in relationship with Messiah Jesus we might have a right relationship with God. (Author's paraphrase of 2 Corinthians 5:21)"

- By accepting Messiah Jesus as your mediator with God you are made right with God and your lack of love is forgiven.

There is a free relationship offered that we need to receive

- At death God will justly judge people for failing to love as they should love. Only those who have accepted the Messiah Jesus as their mediator will be forgiven their lack of love and reconciled to God's love. To be in right relationship with God one must receive the love of God that has been made incarnate in the Messiah.

"For God so loved the world, that he gave his only Son, that whoever believes in him should not perish but have eternal life. For God did not send his Son into the world to condemn the world, but in order that the world might be saved through him. Whoever believes in him is not condemned, but whoever does not believe is condemned already, because he has not believed in the name of the only Son of God. (John 3:16-18; see also Psalm 2)"

This is "theology 102". It is the Christian gospel. This good news says that we are given a right relationship with God as a gift of undeserved mercy which God gives to us in the person of the Messiah Jesus.

"For the just judgment of falling short of our responsibility to love is death, but the free gift of God is being eternally embraced, accepted, and loved in Christ Jesus our Lord. (Author's paraphrase of Romans 6:23)"

So when we die we will stand before God and HE will ask us; "Why should I let you into my heaven?"

Some will say; "Because I ....." The key here is that their trust is in something they did. Their trust is in themselves.

Some will say; "Because Jesus died for my sins and is resurrected to be my priest and mediator. Jesus is my one hope of being forgiven my sins." The key here is that their trust is in Messiah Jesus and not in their own efforts.

How would you answer this question?

Now this "Good News" is controversial. The majority of American would disagree with it. But the real question is if it is true.

I believe that it is true. I trust that I am in right relationship with God only because the Messiah Jesus paid for my sins and rose from the dead. Messiah Jesus is now my one mediator with God. I have peace with God through my Lord Jesus.

I would invite you to accept the Messiah Jesus as your mediator and receive a right relationship with God through accepting HIM. Now I understand that you may not feel you have enough information to make such a radical shift in your relationship with God.   I would recommend the following books which are excellent guides in exploring this "theology 102".

1. Basic Christianity (IVP Classics) John Stott (Author), Rick Warren (Foreword)
2. The Answer by Randy Pope (Author)
3. Whatever Happened to the Gospel? David Nicholas

I believe that this perspective on God is worth investigation. So if you are moved to have any interest at all in thinking more about this alternative theory about how to have right relationship with God then I would urge you to read these books.

I would also love to talk to you about this theory and why I believe it is true. You can call me at Living Water Counseling at 954-452-4407 or email me at normwise@bellsouth.net. Put in you're the subject line of your e-mail "Questions on Theology 102". This will allow me to address it in a timely manner. I would love to interact with you on this or other issues you have found interesting from this book.

Now to take advantage of this unconditional relationship with God means not only having faith but knowing how to live by faith. This means that we have to think about how to relate God's story of love into how we relate to ourselves, others, and our circumstances. We will explore this idea as we develop our thoughts and plans about relationships in this book.

I would also recommend that you read the following books if you want to really understand how to take advantage in a practical sense of this grace relationship we have with God in Christ Jesus.

1. *True Spirituality* by Francis Schaeffer

2. *The Cost of Discipleship* by Dietrich Bonhoeffer

3. *The Golden Booklet on the Christian Life* by John Calvin

These books have had a transforming impact on my perspective on how to live by grace and not just know that I am accepted by grace. I urge you to consider reading them and meditating on their message.

What does this have to do with relationships?

Why does how I view my relationship with God have any impact on how I relate to others? The reason is that this can lead us to have either a performance based approach to relationships with ourselves and others or a grace based approach to relationships with others. This can be vital in having healthy interaction with people.

If I accept people based on how they perform then eventually they will fail my expectations. At this point they fall under my condemnation, disgust, and anger. I will begin to isolate myself from them and reject them. I either have to deny their imperfections or be waiting for the day when they will fall off their pedestal into the mud of shame. There can be no stability in such relationships since eventually every human being will fail in some way to do what they should to in a relationship.

If I accept people based on undeserved favor (grace) then I choose to place this person into my life and give them respect and love as gifts. This gift is not based on their performance but simply on my choice to love and respect them.

I can relate to them honestly when they hurt me, seek reconciliation concerning these hurts, and set boundaries with them. However, I never have to threaten to reject them or stop loving them. I entered into the relationship knowing the person I was choosing to love was imperfect at loving and would need my forgiveness. This realistic expectation allows me then to treat them with patience, empathy, and compassion. This can form stable and long lasting relationships.

My wife and I at our marriage ceremony based our relationship on the following verse of the Bible.

"Accept one another, then, for the glory of God, as Christ has accepted you. " (Romans 15:7)

Jesus the Messiah has accepted us not on the basis of our performance but on the basis of HIS unconditional love and undeserved favor. Since this was how we were accepted by God in Christ Jesus then it makes sense that now we should accept each other on the same basis. For Terry and me, the "Good News" is not just about how to have a right relationship with God but is how to have a right relationship with every person.

This also means that I choose to give unconditional love to myself. I accept myself by grace alone. I will confess when I cause harm to myself or others, set boundaries for my behavior when I see it is harmful, and forgive myself when I do wrong. However, I never reject, hate, or abhor my being. I can hate what I do but not who God has made me. This outlook also provides a stable basis for maintaining a good and realistic self image.

So strangely enough, our theology about how God relates to us can have a huge impact on how we relate to ourselves and others. Despite what our modern world believes; theology matters. The "story" we tell ourselves about God can greatly impact how we interact with others and ourselves.

Now it is true as many of my friends who do not believe in God will point out that just having faith in God does not lead to people treating other people in kind ways.   But, this is because the people who do this are acting inconsistent with a healthy view of God. We must not only believe in God but actually apply a healthy faith in a healthy way for it to make us sane in our relationship with others.

So the foundation to being prepared to have successful and healthy relationships with other people and with the circumstances of my life really are found in developing a sane, stable, and spiritual perception of myself and properly relating to God through the Messiah Jesus.

Now this "knowledge" of God and myself must be more than just "head knowledge" and must be an actual experience of having a true, balanced, and realistic perspective that guides my feelings. As we develop a strategy to improve relationships we will have to build them upon a healthy relationship with our own souls and with God.

One of the key ideas here is that the struggles we are having in our relationships with other people are really only a reflection of how effectively we are relating to spiritual and psychological issues inside of ourselves. Many times our abusive behavior is simply a reflection of attitudes like, shame, guilt, fear, and self righteousness. Only when these inner attitudes change will our ability to relate to others in a sane manner also change.

Now as previously stated; many people who have accepted the Christian "gospel" are still very abusive to other people. That is true. Many people say they will relate to God on the basis of the grace found in Christ Jesus but then relate to others based on self righteousness judgment and abusive behavior. Their faith in the gospel has never changed how they relate to people.

This does not make the gospel false. It just means that if you don't apply truth to a situation then it does not help you. Where Christians do apply the principles of gospel inspired love and grace then relationships do improve.

For those of us who say we accept "theology 102" then it is important that we don't fail to apply it consistently into every relationship. If we say we are saved by God's mercy and grace then we should be a forgiving, kind, patient, and compassionate people. These attitudes reflect what we proclaim we believe about God. It is important that we develop a lifestyle that is consistent with the gospel of unconditional love that we say we believe.

Reflective Questions

1. How important is your relationship with God practically in your daily life? On a scale from 1-10 with 1 being almost no importance to 10 being of primary importance rate realistically your experience of being in an intimate relationship with God.

2. Do you approach God on the basis of your own performance or as a free gift? How do you think this approach to God helps or hinders your relationships to others?

Chapter Three:

Twelve Key Beliefs for developing Healthy Relationships

Relationships are impacted by our words, actions, and attitudes. If our words, actions, and attitudes are hurtful, twisted, and polluted then these will negatively impact every relationship in our life. Where do our words, actions, and attitudes come from?

They come out of a group of beliefs, worldviews, principles, life commandments, personal proverbs, and values that we have developed. Ultimately the only way to change our words, actions, and attitudes so that they will be more healthful than hurtful is to challenge our current "paradigm" or perspective on life. If we will not question what we believe about God, ourselves, others, and the world then our words, actions, and attitudes will never change from what they are today. Lasting change only comes when we change our point of view.

There are twelve key beliefs that have been found by rational philosophical counselors to be significant in developing a healthy perspective on life. I have adapted these twelve key beliefs within my Christian world view. It is only by thinking through each of these twelve beliefs and adapting our convictions around a true view of reality that we will be able to approach relationships successfully. The right beliefs will create healthy words, actions, and attitudes while the wrong beliefs will produce destructive results.

What are these twelve key beliefs?

Carefully and slowly read the key healthy beliefs and the contrasting false beliefs. Honestly mark any of the unhealthy beliefs that you trust in. Put a percentage of trust in each belief box representing how much faith you have in each idea.

It is easy for us to have confliction inside about these issues. Be honest. You can only solve a problem that you admit you have. Once we have identified which beliefs may need to change in your life then we can begin a process of developing a new perspective by which you can produce better words, actions, and attitudes which will help improve relationships in your life.

Healthy Beliefs	Unhealthy Beliefs
1. I cannot make anyone love me but I can choose to love others. I can be sane, stable, and spiritual even if no one chooses to love me. I can enjoy and value the love of others without needing it to survive.	1. I can make people love me by what I do or what I give. My life is not worth living unless others love me. I cannot be sane, stable, or spiritual without others loving me.
2. I can love and respect people who behave poorly. I can love and respect myself when I behave poorly.	2. I cannot love or respect people who behave poorly. I cannot love or respect myself when I behave poorly.
3. Circumstances and events will not be as I would like them. This is normal. I need to focus my energy on changing what I can to make things better. I need to accept what is outside my control as part of God's plan for my life. I need to distinguish what is and what is not under my control realistically.	3. If circumstances and events are not as I like them then life is horrible and I cannot be happy. I will be angry, bitter, and depressed until circumstances change. I will feel guilt over things entirely outside of my control. I will blame others and circumstances for my actions which are under my control.
4. My anxiety is largely caused by the view I take of circumstances and events. It is the "story' I tell about circumstances and events that creates worry, stress, and fear. I can control my emotional state if I control the "interpretive story" I tell myself about life. If I do this I can avoid destructive emotions and encourage constructive emotions in response to the circumstances and events of my life.	4. My anxiety is caused by external circumstances and events and is forced on me. I have no control over feeling worry, stress, and fear. My anxieties are produced by others and by circumstances. I have virtually no control over my emotions. Constructive emotions just come upon me for no reason. I have no control over my happiness.

5. I have a right to be who I am, feeling what I feel, and thinking what I think. Others have a right to be who they are, feel what they feel, and think what they think. Adults have a right to disagree. I do not expect others to agree with me and am able to accept them with our disagreements. We can dialogue in search for truth but I will not hurt someone to force agreement.	5. Everyone should be as I am, feel like I feel, and think like I think. If they disagree with me I must get them to change by causing them pain. I cannot accept people who are different than me. I will abandon and reject everyone who is different.

6. I live in a world in which there are some things that are dangerous and fearsome. I should take prudent actions that will keep me from being at a high risk of harm. I must accept the truth that God is my protector ultimately and rest in HIM to get me through life.	6. If anything is or may be dangerous and fearsome I should be terribly upset and endlessly obsess about it. I must give in to our fears and let them guide us in making decisions. I will see the devil as more active in my life than God.
7. It is better to confront and accept difficulties and responsibilities instead of avoiding them. I accept that I am 100% responsible for what I do, say, and my attitudes. I am assertive and proactive in dealing with life.	7. It is better to avoid difficulties and responsibilities whenever possible. I look to find the "easy way" out of difficult situations and try to get around problems instead of solving them. I blame others for my words, actions, and attitudes.
8. Believe that God has an ultimate purpose for my life and that all my pain has gain.	8. Life is ruled by chaos. There is not purpose or plan. My pain is in vain.
9. Believe that God uses broken	9. Good things can only come to

people. I live by God's grace alone which is found in Messiah Jesus. I accept myself as the imperfect, limited, and fallible child of God. It is direction not perfection that matters. It is part of life to grow, learn, and change. This is a normal part of life. I can learn from the mistakes I made in the past. If I confess my sins to God I will be forgiven and can move forward in life.	me when I have been perfect. I believe I will succeed if I am competent, intelligent, and super achieving in all I do. It is perfection that counts not direction. I cannot admit my mistakes because that would mean we were wrong. My self esteem and self acceptance is based on my never being wrong. I never feel forgiven over anything I have done wrong and live in denial, shame and guilt
10. I do not control other people or circumstances at all. They are outside my control and yet I can enjoy life.	10. I can only be happy when the circumstances and people in my life are under my control.
11. The goal of my life is to fulfill my godly passions, use my God given abilities, and take advantage of my God given opportunities to live a life that glorifies God.	11. The goal of my life is to have enough resources to do nothing everyday and be free of responsibilities.
12. The gospel of Messiah Jesus teaches me that grace, mercy, and tenderness must be at the core of all I do. I choose to be longsuffering, patient, and forgiving towards those who have hurt me.	12. I judge others by my moral law and condemn them for their failures. I see myself as living right and feel angry towards those who are not living right. I am bitter towards those who have hurt me.

We will now look at each of these twelve critical beliefs in depth and see if we can increase our trust in each perspective on life. If we can gain the right perspective then this will help us to approach relationship with a positive mental attitude which will enhance our potential of success in every relationship.

First key belief needed to have sane relationships

1. I cannot make anyone love me but I can choose to love others. I can be sane, stable, and spiritual even if no one chooses to love me. I can enjoy and value the love of others without needing it to survive.	1. I can make people love me by what I do or what I give. My life is not worth living unless others love me. I cannot be sane, stable, or spiritual without others loving me.

Now it is understood that children before the age of ten need nurturing and caring adults to provide for them positive care in order to develop in a healthy way. Children can be seriously wounded and scarred by abuse, neglect, and rejection. Adults have a special responsibly to give them a loving and secure relationship.

But once we are adults we have the ability to begin to heal from such emotional wounds of the past. I also must recognize the reality that I cannot view my sanity, stability, or spirituality as depending on other people. Not even my parents. I must accept full responsibility for my own inner peace and realize that I do not have the power to make people love me. I only have the power to choose to love others. By doing this, I can receive the love of others without becoming dependent upon it for my survival.

We feel more secure believing that we can make people love us by what we say, do, or become. This gives us a sense of control over an issue vital to us. We believe that our inner well being depends on us having the love, acceptance, and appreciation of others. This makes us very vulnerable, fragile, and likely to take radical actions to save relationships. Rarely do radical actions lead to good results.

A co-dependent relationship is one where I believe that by doing what the other person wants me to do they will accept and love me. I do not set healthy boundaries. I will not refuse to be treated in an abusive manner. My life and happiness become dependent upon their acceptance of me. Without them I cannot be "OK".

If I find that I am dependent on people in this way I need to put this first true belief on a 3 by 5 card and read it six times a day for ninety days. I should read it out loud so that I can hear it. I must begin to reprogram my mind with a new belief. I must also begin to recognize that my actions do not make anyone love me.

In addition here are four steps to take in a relationship where you have felt that you could make someone love you and have attempted to specifically do things that would create love for you in that relationship.

Step one: Speak the truth to the person instead of what they want to hear. Tell them what you really think and feel in a loving and non-abusive manner. Truth does not have to be rude but it does have to be candid. Real relationships are based on telling each other what we really think and feel and not just telling people what we believe they want us to say. I need to speak in a kind way but with real integrity.

Step two - Set up reasonable boundaries in the relationship. A boundary is where you say "no" when you feel you should say "no" instead of saying "yes" just to get the other person to approve of you. This "no" should be one that reflects your thoughts and feelings and not just done arbitrarily. The key here is that you are willing to not compromise your principles, beliefs, and values just to gain the other person's appreciation.

Step Three - Stand your ground once you begin to redefine this relationship. Many times people will negatively respond to us ending a co-dependent relationship because it has made them the center of our lives. They may not have given us love in response to our actions but they enjoyed being the focus so much energy.

They may well say "What is wrong with you?" or "What has gotten into you?" You need to share with them in a gentle and kind way the positive feelings you have for them but that you had put them in a position that only God should have in your life. You are just attempting to make your relationship healthier and more balanced.

Don't blame them for anything because this really was about your wrong beliefs. Explain you are just making some adjustments and reassure them that you are not rejecting them. Tell them "I believed that I could make you care about me now I see that this is something you alone can choose to do."

Make sure however than you are not just expressing built up anger and frustration and calling it a "boundary." You should continue to do positive things in the relationships which are healthy expressions of your love for them but only set boundaries where needed. Choose to do random acts of kindness to them but without any expectation of a good reaction from them. Remember, you can choose to act in loving ways whenever you desire just not believe that you can create love in another person. Our desire here is not to hurt anyone one but to regain a healthy balance in our own thinking.

However, don't relapse into just doing things to try to get a good reaction from them. Remember they can choose to either love you or not love you. That is their choice.

Step four – Balance your life and learn to nurture yourself outside the relationship. Tell yourself "This relationship is part of my life and is not my life". Spend time with other friends and family. Learn how to enjoy time alone. Treat yourself to your favorite food or recreational activity. Recognize that while there is joy in this relationship that is not the only joy you have in life.

Now if we have based most of the relationships in our lives on the false belief we can make people love us it may take us some time to overcome this pattern. That is alright. Time is our friend.

We did not get into destructive beliefs and behavior overnight and normally it will take us time to adjust ourselves to reality. But with focus, prayer, and practice we can find ourselves becoming more and freer of co-dependency and enjoying healthy relationships with other adults.

Reflective Questions

1. Who are the people in your life that you have a tendency to feel that you could not live without them?

2. Why is it hard to think about choosing to love another person with no guarantee or promise you will be loved in return?

3. Do you think you have any relationships in your life that are "co-dependent" and need to become healthy adult to adult relationships? If so which ones and how would you move these relationships into becoming more healthy?

Second key belief need to have successful relationships

2. I can love and respect people who behave poorly. I can love and respect myself when I behave poorly.	2. I cannot love or respect people who behave poorly. I cannot love or respect myself when I behave poorly.

"Accept one another, then, for the glory of God, as Christ has accepted you." (Romans 15:7)

Many people base relationships on performance. We decide that people have to earn our love and respect. We even decide that we have to earn our own love and respect. Love and respect are not gifts we give but rewards we offer.

The problem is that in the long run no human beings will meet our expectations. Every human being fails in their responsibilities in some way and at some time. Everyone falls short of our standards of performance.

The other problem here is that this uses our "love" as a carrot at the end of a stick. We are using the promise or potential of our giving our love and respect as a way to get people to do what we want. This makes our love manipulative and at times even cruel. Our focus becomes on having "power and control" in the relationship instead of a real unconditional commitment of love in the relationships. We could fear giving our love and respect to anyone because then we are afraid that people will not do what we want. Performance based relationships are always abusive and never healthy.

If we see our love and respect as rewards to be given to those who perform, we will find that we do not love or respect anyone for long. At critical points we will find that we don't live up to our own expectations and this will lead us to despise and abuse ourselves. When we base love and respect of people on performance we will live in a world of disappointment, bitterness, and despair. No one has ever escaped this reality in human relationships.

I must decide to love and respect people for who they are and not for what they do. The people in my life are made in God's image and therefore deserve my respect and love. I need to treat them in an honoring and respectful manner for they have been "fearfully and wonderfully" made by the Creator. I need to love them because God loves them. I need to respect them because God respects them. Human beings are sacred and been set apart by God as the most significant part of HIS creation.

I must see myself in this same light. I must decide to love and respect myself because God has love and respect for me. I must value my own being because I believe that at core I am a special and sacred creation of God. This demonstrates again how what we believe about God can impact how we relate to people.

Now human beings are also sinners. This means that they do immoral actions, say immoral things, and have immoral attitudes. We fail to love as we ought to love. We don't always do the right things and we take actions that are wrong. At times we fail to take positive actions we should take and at others we do hurtful things that should never have been done. We should feel guilt over these moral transgressions. But guilt is not self hatred. It is not a rejection of who God has made us.

Healthy guilt is a sense of embarrassment and remorse over what I have done not a hating of who I am. It is the recognition that I owed God, my fellow human being, and myself; more love than I gave. Guilt is deep regret over a failure to do my duty in a relationship. But guilt is not despising who God made me, abusing myself, or wishing I had never been born.

We can hold ourselves and others accountable without failing to love and honor them. We do not have to abuse people or fail to love them in order to set healthy boundaries with them. Love has boundaries. It does mean that we recognize that every person deserves to be treated in a healthy and non-abusive manner because they are sacred to God. It is important how we define a human being. If we have a wrong definition of human beings then we will treat people wrong every time we act on our beliefs about individuals.

Now I must have realistic expectations about human beings. Here are some realistic expectations to have in our human relationships.

- Every human being who loves me will hurt me because they are a sinner.
- Every human being who loves me will bless me because they are made in God's image
- Every human being I love, I will hurt because I am a sinner.
- Every human being I love, I will bless because I am made in God's image

We can either accept this reality or be surprised every time we experience it. What we see as inconsistency in people is really just their dual nature as reflecting the divine image and being rebels against God. Every human being is like this. Therefore we should expect it. If we will only love and respect those who are perfect, we will be in a healthy relationship with no one.

Now the gospel of Messiah Jesus again helps us to know how to respond to this difficult reality.

"For while we were still weak, at the right time Christ died for the ungodly. For one will scarcely die for a righteous person--though perhaps for a good person one would dare even to die-- but God shows his love for us in that while we were still sinners, Christ died for us."
(Romans 5:6-8)

God chose to love us when we were weak, ungodly, and still sinners. He decided to sacrifice HIMSELF in order to establish a relationship with us. He honored us and had compassion for us at our worst. His love for us was not deserved or earned. It as a free gift.

God wants us to see in HIS actions an attitude we should copy. As he treated us with grace and mercy so we should also treat others with grace and mercy.

"Let all bitterness and wrath and anger and clamor and slander be put away from you, along with all malice. Be kind to one another, tenderhearted, forgiving one another, as God in Christ forgave you. "
(Ephesians 4:31-32)

So since God has accepted, loved, and respected us in our sinful state so we are also to accept, love, and respect each other in our imperfect condition. The gospel tells us to love broken people because God loves broken people.

Now for some of us the hardest person for us to love is ourselves. Our inner world is full of verbal and emotional abuse we afflict upon our own souls. We believe that by hating, rejecting, and denying ourselves self approval we will become better people. This has never worked in anyone's life. A poor self image does not lead to a healthy life.

The gospel can also help us with acceptance of ourselves.

".... whenever our heart condemns us, God is greater than our heart, and he knows everything." (1 John 3:20)

When we begin our self condemnation for our failures then we need to preach the gospel to ourselves and remind our inner being that nothing can separate us from the love of God that is in Christ Jesus. We need to remember that God is not condemning us in Christ Jesus and that God has forgiven us so we should forgive ourselves.

If we are to have long lasting and stable relationships with others we must understand that this will require many acts of reconciliation, forgiveness, mercy, patience, and long suffering. We will have to look at the glass half full and know that we have decided to love a sinful, weak, and broken person. We need to keep realistic expectations concerning what they will do.

Now the same is true with anyone that will remain with us in the long run because we also are weak and broken people. The only friends we will have in the long run are those who decide to love and respect us despite our faults. All human relationships depend on acceptance of each other in our weak and sinful condition.

If this is a key issue for you and you struggle with this second key belief then reviewing it on a 3X5 card for ninety days may begin to help you let go of your unrealistic expectations. Think carefully about the impossibility of anyone earning your love and respect. Appreciate the fact that others knowing that you are far from perfect have chosen to love and respect you. Over time you should find yourself more and more able to see that the love and respect you are giving are free gifts and not rewards for good behavior.

The key here is that we begin to accept reality about others and ourselves. We will at times act poorly and those in our life will act poorly. If we are to love and honor people we must do this in the context of accepting people with their poor behavior.

Reflective Questions

1. How could you bring grace into relationships that are dominated by condemnation, abandonment, and rejection today?

2. How can you apply your faith in the love God has for you in the sacrifice of Christ for your sins with in such a way that you will be more able to love and accept yourself?

Third key belief need to have sane relationships

3. Circumstances and events will not be as I would like them. This is normal. I need to focus my energy on changing what I can to make things better. I need to accept what is outside my control as part of God's plan for my life. I need to distinguish what is and what is not under my control realistically.	3. If circumstances and events are not as I like them then life is horrible and I cannot be happy. I will be angry, bitter, and depressed until circumstances change. I will feel guilt over things entirely outside of my control. I will blame others and circumstances for my actions which are under my control.

The Serenity Prayer

God grant me the serenity
to accept the things I cannot change;
courage to change the things I can;
and wisdom to know the difference.

Living one day at a time;
Enjoying one moment at a time;
Accepting hardships as the pathway to peace;
Taking, as He did, this sinful world
as it is, not as I would have it;
Trusting that He will make all things right
if I surrender to His Will;
That I may be reasonably happy in this life
and supremely happy with Him
Forever in the next.
Amen.

--Reinhold Niebuhr

Most of us have been waiting for the people in our lives and the circumstances of our life to be "good" so that we can be happy. We blame our unhappiness upon the fact that neither the people in our lives or our circumstances have ever been as we liked them to be. Whatever brief moments of happiness most people have are when they have moments when the people and events in their lives lined up with their expectations.

Not only must I accept imperfect people I have to accept very imperfect circumstances in my life. Life will have difficulties, loses, and frustrations. I will feel at times homeless, powerless, rootless, hopeless, and meaningless. I will lose jobs, have loved ones die, suffer betrayal by friends and family, and see my best efforts fail. Some of my most loves dreams will not be fulfilled. Life is hard.

How can a hard life be managed? How can one have good relationships when suffering so many things that are painful and difficult? If so much is outside of our control then what is under our control?

The key principle here is to down at the core of our being accept the reality that the only thing we have under our control is our words, our actions and our attitudes. As long as we can blame others for "making us lose our temper" and for taking actions which were abusive then we can never have any control. We will never control what others do or the vast majority of circumstances in our lives and if these things outside of us control us, then none of us have any control at all.

As long as my inner contentment is based on what others do and what happens in my life then I will never be able to live a sane, stable, and spiritual life. If my ability to love people depends on what happens to me and on how they act, then I really have no independent ability to love people at all. There would not be any "unconditional love" if all of my love depends on the actions of others and if my circumstances are comfortable. In such a case all love would be very fragile.

One of the core motivations for anger is unmet expectations. If I think I can control others and circumstances, I will get frustrated when I they don't do what I want. This will lead to me taking abusive, manipulative, and angry actions as I strive to control what they say and do. This destroys relationships. If I know that the actions of other people and most circumstances are outside my control, then my expectations become less and with this I feel less anger. This actually helps me maintain self control and choose a response that is healthy for the circumstances.

For example here are some false beliefs which can lead us into false expectations and elevated states where we can "explode" in anger and hurt the people we love the most.

- If you work hard the you will have financial success
- If you play by the rules you will win
- If you love people they will love you back
- My spouse will never lie to me
- My children will appreciate all I sacrifice and love me for what I do for them

Many of us have "life proverbs" that tell us that if we do something it will make other people react to us in a particular way. This is not true. We never have control of others but at most can gain control of ourselves.

Learning Contentment

"Not that I am speaking of being in need, for I have learned in whatever situation I am to be content. I know how to be brought low, and I know how to abound. In any and every circumstance, I have learned the secret of facing plenty and hunger, abundance and need. I can do all things through him who strengthens me." (Philippians 4:11-13 ESV)

"Now there is great gain in godliness with contentment, for we brought nothing into the world, and we cannot take anything out of the world."
(1 Timothy 6:6-7 ESV)

What is contentment? It is to want today what I have today. To be able to accept what I have as Gods' will for today and not expect more than what I have.

Now these verses do mean that I will embrace my current financial situation and not become angry, depressed, or anxious over the physical status of my life. But the idea is bigger than that. These verses also imply that I should accept the real state of my relationships, the decisions that people make today, and who they are today. I will not be expecting them to be different but will simply strive to understand what reality is and then adapt to it.

One man felt that to be able to love his family he had to provide an upper middle class income them. When his business was doing well he would act in kind and loving ways towards his wife and children. However, to achieve this he felt he had to work very long hours and so there was not a lot of time to enjoy with them. If his business did poorly and money was tight he would become angry, frustrated, and avoid his family. He felt unworthy to be a husband and father if he was not able to provide for his family a good income. So when his business did well he worried that it would do poorly tomorrow and had little time for his family and if his business did poorly he felt unworthy to be loved as a father and dad, so avoided his family until things got turned around. Clearly a lack of contentment and bad ideas about money hurt his relationships. Our feelings, beliefs, and fears about finances do impact our relationships.

But we can struggle with a lack of contentment in many other ways outside of finances. For instance if my teenager has never cleaned their room, regardless of what I have said to them, then for me to expect that today when I walk into the room that things will be clean is an unrealistic expectation. If I throw a tantrum and act shocked at their room being a mess, I may get a little better cleaning of the room but normally at a very high cost to the relationship. However, it does not change anything really and in a couple of days I have to be ready to throw another tantrum to get the room cleaned and the impact of this emotional explosion is less than my first one because my teenager is getting use to me being crazy and is less scared. So the returns are diminishing in getting the room clean and increasing as far as hurting the relationship.

So what can I do if I don't try to use a tantrum and moral shock at the room being a mess? What would a loving and logical parent do in response to a messy room? That is the key question.

I can learn to be content with the reality that my teenager has not yet learned the skill of cleaning their room. My role as parent is to train them to do this and to develop ways to help them learn this. This is my duty and task in relationship with my child. I need to teach them how to do this in a way that communicates love and respect for them. So I face reality, define my role, and then can joyfully approach this task without a tantrum.   There is no cause and effect relationship between a messy room and an explosion of anger. I can choose to respond in whatever way I think would be best for my child and me.

But how can I learn to be content?

The Greek word for contentment found in the New Testament is "autarkeia" and the best definition of the term seems to be "a mental independence from all circumstances". Strangely enough this comes back to our vision of God again. If I believe that God is at work in all my circumstances even when they are painful, disappointing, and destructive then the worst days of my life become less fearful. If I believe that there is no divine plan behind these events and chaos rules life, then my fear, frustration, panic, and anger rise.   The circumstances do not change but my response to the circumstances does change.

For example, in World War II there were many prisoners in the Nazi concentration camps. There was a great deal one could become bitter about in such camps where abuse, injustice, and pain abounded. One of the daily torments of the prisoners was that the barracks in which they lived were filled with fleas.   One group of prisoners was at one end of the barracks cursing, complaining, and even expressing anger at God over how the fleas made their lives miserable. At the other end of the barracks there was a group of prisoners huddled together in prayer. Among their prayers was one of "thanks" for "brother flea". Now why would they thank God for "brother flea"?

Well because of the fleas the one place the guards would not enter was the barracks. This made the barracks the safest place in the camp and where there was the greatest freedom to talk.   Both groups suffered from the same fleas, but one group had learned to be content and the other had not yet reached this conclusion.

So part of becoming content is to believe there is a purpose behind all my pain and trust that none of my pain will be wasted. This is an attitude of faith. But with such an attitude deeply grounded into the very core of our being, it can help us to respond in more positive ways to the circumstances of our life. This means that we will be expressing more sane, stable, and spiritual words and actions when we deal with the people we love. This allows us to have a positive influence on the relationships that we value.

To be content, I must become solution focused instead of problem focused. I must not keep telling myself how I wish things were, but instead ask myself what I can do to make them better. What can I practically do to improve things? Now what I say I can do need to be realistic but this is where my focus needs to be instead of simply becoming upset and angry over what I do not have.

For example I can be upset that my spouse does not love me more. This is outside my control. I do not control if my spouse loves me or how much they love me. I can control how much I express love to them. I can choose to express kindness, understanding, and a desire to listen.

By doing this I can create an atmosphere where it is easier for my spouse to express love. This is something I can do and put my energy into without any expectation that it will lead to any particular results. It simply must be done because it is the right thing to do and can make me more healthy in my relationship with my spouse.

Now I can have a preferred future that I can hope for and in which I know that I would take pleasure if it was reached. However, I must never make my contentment dependent on reaching this preferred future. I must not say I can be "happy" only when circumstances change since that means that my happiness is dependent on a fragile set of circumstances that could change.

Instead, I have to live for today, knowing I am agnostic about the future, and seek to respond to my circumstances in a sane, stable, and spiritual way. If I do this then my happiness is not dependent on things changing but simply on my changing inwardly in dealing with what I have to face in a mature, logical, and loving manner. Happiness becomes my choice as I face a difficult and uncertain life.

It is important that I know the difference between the "ideal relationship" and the "real relationship". The "ideal relationship" whether that be the "ideal marriage", the "ideal child", or the "ideal boss" exist only in my mind. There are no ideal people or relationships. Real people relating to other real people bring into that mix both their vices and virtues.

Each person brings the baggage they have from other relationships and experiences into every other connection they have with other people. So if I will be unhappy and dissatisfied with any relationship outside the "ideal" then I have predetermined that I will be unhappy, discontented, frustrated, and angry in every relationship. We must be content with the "real relationships" we have with "real people" who are made up of flaws, failures, promise, and potential. We must avoid "black and white" thinking and instead learn to enjoy living in a world of "grey".

Now to achieve this means that I will need to learn to nurture my soul in a way that I will have the physical, emotional, and spiritual strength to control my words, actions, and attitudes. Many times we are attempting to have good relationships with others in a state of constant exhaustion. Exhausted people make mistakes. So learning to nurture ourselves is an important part of preparing ourselves to successfully relate to others. We need to have a plan each day that includes some time for self reflection, exercise, prayer, and biblical meditation. We need to establish a "rule of life" in which we seek to find God's peace, presence, and power so we can live the day in a sane, stable, and spiritual manner.

For further reading on this topic I would recommend.

Finding Contentment: When Momentary Happiness Just Isn't Enough by Neil Clark Warren

The Secret of Contentment by William B. Barcley

The Art of Divine Contentment by Thomas Watson

The key belief here is to clearly see that I have no control over the other people in my life and limited control over the circumstances of my life. My happiness, sanity, stability, and spirituality cannot depend on what they do or don't do. Instead, I have to depend on God's plan for my life and put my energy on living a life ruled by love and logic in every decision, word, action, and attitude I have. This is all I really have control over and how I can have the most positive influence on every relationship in my life.

Reflective Questions

1. Who in your life do you want to have power and control over the most? In what relationships do you put the most pressure on people to conform to your will? What motivates you to do this?

2. To what extent do you accept the idea that you are 100% responsible for your words, actions, and attitudes? Do you ever blame others for what you do? How do you think you could accept more responsibility for what you say, do, and feel?

3. What makes it hard to be content in your current circumstances? Do you think anyone has your circumstances and is more content than you are?

Fourth key belief need to have sane relationships

4. My anxiety is largely caused by the view I take of circumstances and events. It is the "story' I tell about circumstances and events that creates worry, stress, and fear. I can control my emotional state if I control the "interpretive story" I tell myself about life. If I do this I can avoid destructive emotions and encourage constructive emotions in response to the circumstances and events of my life.	4. My anxiety is caused by external circumstances and events and is forced on me. I have no control over feeling worry, stress, and fear. My anxieties are produced by others and by circumstances. I have virtually no control over my emotions. I cannot help feeling many destructive emotions that lead to destructive actions. Constructive emotions just come upon me for no reason. I have no control over my happiness.

"The destiny of the world is determined less by the battles that are lost and won than by the stories it loves and believes in."
—Harold Goddard

One of the unique aspects of humanity is that we are story tellers. From the beginning of human history people would sit around fires and tell stories. Some of the stories would be about what had happened, others would be tales about things that might have happened, and some were words which created worlds that never had existed but that now inspired us to live well in this world.

Most of the Bible, the best read book in the world, is stories about God and people. Stories and people were made for each other. God is a story teller and because we are like God we tell stories to make sense of life.

If you put ten people in a room around a table and they begin talking to each other, you know that it will not be long before someone is telling a story in order to entertain, instruct, or inspire the others. Our minds operate and think in stories. Out of the stories of our minds we live, act, and feel.

Every person has two primary emotions. One is pain and the other pleasure. We normally attempt to avoid or limit the pain we feel and strive to maximize the pleasure. Now events have "knee jerk" levels of pain or pleasure associated with them. If someone gives me a compliment I normally feel pleasure, if they curse me I feel pain, If a person kisses me, I feel pleasure, and if they slap me I feel pain. This is what I would call "level 1" experience of pain or pleasure and it is automatic, natural, and healthy. If we don't experience pain and pleasure in this normal way to stimulus then this usually means there is something severely wounded in us physically or emotionally.

But in addition to this "level one" pain or pleasure there is a deeper pain or pleasure we feel due to experiences we have. This could be called "level two" pain or pleasure. "Level two" pain or pleasure is the story I use to interpret whatever it is I am experiencing. This story is part of a "life narrative" which I use to make sense of everything in my life. Each experience and event I weave into my "life narrative" at a conscious and subconscious level so I can make sense of everything that happens in my life.

For example someone kisses me. The physical experience of a kiss normally produces pleasure. Now, if the story I have around this kiss is "this kiss means they love me!" then my pleasure will increase and expand. However, if my story is "their just kissing me to use me" or "they are just kissing me because they cannot kiss someone else they really love" then the kiss becomes "painful". Same kiss but different story about the kiss created by the stories we tell about it change an experience of pleasure into an experience of pain.

Now stories can be true or false, optimistic or pessimistic, or realistic or illusionary. Many of the stories we tell about events are "half truths" which ignore vital facts. While some people are "Polly Anna", naïve, and overly positive most of us tend to be overly cynical, pessimistic, and negative. Most people have made more dark predictions about their lives and relationships that have never come true. The majority of us have told ourselves many more negative stories that predicted some disaster than positive predictions about the future.

Our aim should be to tell ourselves a truthful and healthy story about what has occurred. The goal would be to have our "story" about an event imitate what we would imagine God's story would be about what has occurred. By telling myself the true story about whatever I experience, then my emotions are healthy and balanced.

We relate to people based on "the scripts" we have going on in our heads. A husband cleans the house and the wife interprets it as "he just attempting to get me in bed" or "he is trying to tell me that I don't clean the house well." In both cases the cleaning of the house will create pain, fear, frustration and even anger. Many times a spouse will not even share their interpretation and so their negative response to a positive action is a complete mystery to the other person. This leads us to "mind reading" people so that we think we know what motivates another person without asking them. A wife can plan a romantic evening and the husband can interpret it as "what does she want now?" or "what did she do wrong that she is trying to make up for?" So a positive action by the wife becomes a painful experience for the husband. Normally such negative responses are a mystery to the other spouse and this then leads to other "stories" being told in order to make sense of a negative response to positive actions.

Now our "life stories" begin when we are children. Before the age of ten we observe, absorb, and process in our basic "life narrative". To the degree we suffer abuse, trauma, and discord during these early years then our interpretation of life will be one of mistrust, shame, doubt, unrealistic guilt, and inferiority. To the extent we experienced nurture, care, and unconditional love; the interpretation of life reflects trust, self control, initiative, realistic guilt, forgiveness, and a balanced work ethic.

As we strive to begin to relate to each other in relationships as adults we bring into these relationships and experiences the "life story" that we developed as children. This "life story" developed by us as children, become an "interpretive grid" or "lenses" through which we see everything. This is why it is vital that we make peace with our past, rewrite the programming we received as children, and carefully develop the "life story" that we will live by if we are to be successful in our relationships.

Most people catch their life story the way we catch the common cold. We pick it up somewhere in our environment. Most people also have never thought that they are "interpreting" life they think that the way they see things is "just the ways things are" and that it is the only perspective one can have in understanding events.

This is why when people have very different "life stories" and interpret life differently they have such a hard time understanding each other. We see the other person's interpretation of events as "stupid" or "absurd". We have a very hard time having empathy for how others view the world. This conflict can lead us to having deep feelings of frustration, fear, and anger towards those who see things differently than we do.

So I need to understand that as an adult I need to know my "life story" through which I am interpreting the world and decide if it is a healthy way to interpret life and relationships or if I need to change it. I have the ability as an adult to rewrite my "life story" and change my perspective on how I see things. By doing this I can have a healthier response to struggles I have with people and events.

I would recommend the following books on developing a healthier life story.

1. Scripts People Live: Transactional Analysis of Life Scripts by Claude Steiner

2. Broken Children, Grown-Up Pain (Revised): Understanding the Effects of Your Wounded Past by Paul Hegstrom

2. Healing the Hardware of the Soul: Enhance Your Brain to Improve Your Work, Love, and Spiritual Life by Dr. Daniel Amen

3. Man's Search for Meaning: An Introduction to Logotherapy by Viktor E. Frankl

4. What Would Aristotle Do? Self-Control Through the Power of Reason by Elliot D. Cohen

5. Succeeding at Life by Dr. Norman Wise

Now all books have to be read with discernment and an open Bible. But these books could help provide for you a good set of tools by which you could effectively begin to rewrite your life story. They have within them some good ideas that can help you learn how to reprogram your mind.

Take time to listen to yourself when you are under pressure. Whenever the pain or pleasure of your life is extreme then what is the story you are telling yourself? How could you alter this story?

Learn to debate yourself whenever your story may not be totally true. How do you know when your life script is not 100% accurate? Here are some key ways to know.

1. Look out for universal statements such as "No one loves me"; "No one understands me"; or "I never do anything right". Universal statements are rarely true but they have a lot more emotional punch. Our "life proverbs" are normally stated in very absolute ways.

One key to rewriting these type of statements is to make them realistic. For example: "Some people love me and some people don't; "Some people get who I am and some people don't get me at all"; "Sometimes I really do well and sometimes I really blow it." Clearly these statements would create different emotions and attitudes than when we state our feelings in absolute and universal ways.

2. Statements that are totally positive or negative while predicting the future normally represent bad life stories. Examples could be "I never will lose"; "I never will win; "This relationship will never lead to either of us being happy"; "You will never change"

One key way to avoid this type of universal and absolute statement is to admit you are agnostic about the future. These are guesses. Restating them might sound like this; "I don't feel it is very likely that I will win, but I will still give it a try." "I feel very good about my chances at winning today, but you never know." "I feel that the probability of our relationship becoming healthy and happy is low, but maybe we can beat the odds."

Notice that our predictions are defined for what they are which is "feelings" since no one knows anything about the future and they are balanced with acknowledging that these "feelings" may be wrong. Also take note that we need to guard against overly optimistic attitudes that can lead to deep disappointment if not fulfilled or a false sense of having control of the future if they happen to occur as we predicted.

3. When we blame others for our actions or take the blame of what others do; then this is not a good life script. This can be as simple as "I have a bad temper because I am Irish"; "There is just something about me that irritates people"; or "If people would just leave me alone I would be fine."

Overcoming this type of life programming means that we need to restate the truth. We would have to contradict ourselves. "I choose to have a bad temper because I like being a hot head. This has nothing to do with me being Irish"; "I have a wonderful personality created by God and some people who are different than me struggle because we are different"; or "My problems are hid better when I don't have to deal with people. I need to start dealing with my issues so that I can relate to people with more love."

The key here is to know your life narrative and whatever is good in it keep but whatever is unhealthy in it get rid of it. Remember, you are now the script writer. Regardless of what script you were given by your parents you now can rewrite it and make it better, healthier, and more effective. This is the ultimate freedom we have in our lives.

Reflective Questions

1. How do you think what you experienced growing up impacts how you interpret events today?   Do you see this as positive or negative in helping you cope with other people and life in general?

2. Is there any particular part of your life script or narrative that you would like to rewrite? How do you think you could rewrite this part of your story?

3.   How would a new "life narrative" help the relationships in your life?

Fifth key belief needed to have sane relationships

5. I have a right to be who I am, feeling what I feel, and thinking what I think. Others have a right to be who they are, feel what they feel, and think what they think. Adults have a right to disagree. I do not expect others to agree with me and am able to accept them with our disagreements. I can dialogue in search for truth but I will not hurt someone to force agreement. I am able to love and respect people who are different than I am, feel different than I feel, and think different than I think.	5. Everyone should be as I am, feel like I feel, and think like I think. If they disagree with me I must get them to change by causing them pain. I cannot accept people who are different than me. I will abandon and reject everyone who is different.

It is very hard to have adult to adult relationships with people. We have a tendency to either want to parent people and treat them as children or to avoid conflict pretend we agree with people when we don't. When we try to dominate others they normally resist and we find ourselves in conflict. If they don't openly resist they resent they are being treated as children and will find indirect ways to overcome the feeling of being dishonored by our domination of them. In time, bitterness towards us can grow and then we can have a very radical, powerful, and destructive explosion in our relationships. These will normally surprise us since we saw everything in the relationship as fine because we were getting our way and minimized the other person's point of view.

Some people have become "chameleons" and in order to avoid conflict have blended into the culture and environment they find themselves living in. They have done this to survive. Conflict was dangerous and they did believe that if they failed to blend in they would be hurt. So they changed their colors and blended into the back ground.

Some "chameleons" have done this so long that they no longer really know who they are, what they feel, or their own thoughts. It can take some time for a person who has been in "chameleon" mode to remember who they are. Any relationships a "chameleon" has are an illusion and can fall apart if that illusion is destroyed or discovered before the "chameleon" is ready to give it up.

Some "mid-life" crisis is caused because a person was living a life of a "chameleon" and either just became aware that they had been living a lie or consciously knew they had a dual personality but decided to end the hypocrisy. In one situation I am aware of a man who was not a Christian, pretended to be a Christian in order to "get the girl" and then after two decades of marriage and raising a family, gave it up to be the "pagan" he always knew he was at heart. Needless to say his children and wife were both hurt very badly. This just demonstrates the danger there is in being in a relationship with a "chameleon" and how important it is that we place personal integrity at the heart of every relationship.

Now "chameleons" normally are tempted to become "chameleons" because there are strong dominating personalities in families that are saying that "it is my way or the high way". They live in a "win/lose" world and they don't want to lose. These strong personalities may only offer conditional love and respect based on performance and has little tolerance for those who don't measure up. Other adults are treated as children and inferior. They are to follow the leader. Civil and honest discussion of different points of view is not allowed. From the "chameleon's point of view they have little choice but to blend in or die.

So we must stress that to have a relationship with people it must be safe for people to be who they are, feel what they feel, and think what they think. This does not mean that all ideas are equally true. But it does mean that an adult has a right to have an opinion and give reasons why they see things that way.

People need to know that those who are family and friends will love and respect them regardless of their personality type, the emotions they are experiencing, or the thought process they currently are exploring. Healthy relationships have honest dialogue in which people speak honestly, humbly, kindly, and with respect with each other. Disagreement is an opportunity for intellectual and relational growth.

Now our theology plays a part of this approach. Every human being is created in the image of God and is therefore worthy of love and respect regardless of what they do. We are see in each person a reflection of the divine attributes and one that has the capacity to reflect God into creation more effectively than any other creatures. If this person is also a Christian then they are a member of God's eternal family, adopted, loved, and cherished by the creator of all things. God has bankrupted heaven to have HIS SON pay for our sins and demonstrate the victory of that sacrifice in HIS resurrection. Every Christian has been bought with a price and is part of the body of CHRIST. We must therefore give to each person the honor they are due and share with them the abundance, warmth, and love they deserve being the objects of God's great care. To curse people is to curse God because they are made in HIS image (James 3:1-10). So it important to recognize that people have a right to be heard, treated with respect, and loved regardless of how much we disagree.

Part of respecting God's image in a person is that we are quick to listen to them, slow to dominate the conversation with our words, and slow to lose our tempers (James 1:19-20). They are worthy to be heard for they are the image bearers of God. Also since God has made them part of our lives then we must assume that HE desires some us to have a dialogue with the ideas they hold to help us move closer to the truth. Our best thinking normally comes in dialogue with other people who are also seeking for the truth. Brain storming is an effective means of showing honor to each other.

Brainstorming: Adult to Adult communication

So when we become aware that different points of views exist; it is good to then make a choice to develop a brainstorming session with the other person and seek first to comprehend the other person and then be understood by the other person, instead of having a hostile argument. In addition to hearing each other the hope of brainstorming includes the idea of everyone growing in their comprehension of the issues and finding a brand new way to look at things. We should not avoid those with whom we disagree but instead seek a space to talk to them.

So the first thing is to make sure everyone feels safe and heard. Allow the other people or person you are brainstorming with to voice their thoughts first. Then give them active feedback on what you hear them say. After they have been heard then also explain your viewpoint and seek feedback from them to make sure you have been heard. People have a great need to be heard so this satisfies a deep need we have. Hearing is not agreeing.

Then raise the question. What are all the different ways that this problem or topic could be approached? Encourage as many ideas as possible, Don't judge ideas but ask what reasons support the idea and what makes it less likely to be true or effective, don't look ahead to making decisions just encourage discussion; Build on one another's ideas, encourage participation from everyone who will be impacted by the discussion.

This can include under the right circumstances. Participation by children adds some novel concepts and going through this process trains them in how to think. This can also help children support a decision if they feel they were part of a process that led up to the decision.

Don't worry about the words used to express ideas but strive to get a good picture of what the person means, and as you go through this process write down the ideas that are discussed. Every thought is honored by being written down and considered. .

If people used brainstorming as the main means of thinking through different points of view instead of going into a "win/lose" mentality in which we have to fight, become angry, and argue then it would make a significant impact. However brainstorming only makes sense if our belief is that adults have a right to disagree and we look at disagreement as an opportunity to grow in our understanding of each other and the topic at hand. It is an open, non-defensive, and safe process in which people can really become a team. This core belief is one of the most critical if people are to effectively communicate to each other.

For those who would like to read some additional things on this process I would recommend:

1. Life Journaling: A Process of Finding Peace in Relationships by Dr. Norman Wise

2. Learning to Love in 27 Days by Dr. Norman Wise

3. I'm OK - You're OK: : A Practical Guide to Transactional Analysis by M.D. Thomas A. Harris

This belief allows us to actually show respect to other people. It is only when we interact with others as equal adults that we truly honor them in their proper role. This also allows our relationships to be free of co-dependency. This is a vital belief to master and apply.

Reflective Questions

1. What makes it hard to accept other adults as equals? Why is it hard to not develop win/lose relationships with people?

2. Do you know any "chameleons"? Are you a "chameleon"? How can you encourage the "chameleons" in your life to show their true colors? If you are a "chameleon" then what can you do to end the game?

Sixth key belief needed to have sane relationships

6. I live in a world in which there are some things that are dangerous and fearsome. I should take prudent actions that will keep me from being at a high risk of harm. I must accept the truth that God is our protector ultimately and rest in HIM to get us through life.	6. If anything is or may be dangerous and fearsome I should be terribly upset and endlessly obsess about it. I must give in to my fears and let them guide me in making decisions. I will see the devil as more active in my life than God.

"I am Wisdom --Common Sense is my closest friend; I possess knowledge and sound judgment." (Proverbs 8:12 CEV)

Humanity now lives "East of Eden". We are not in paradise anymore. Yet, the truth is that God's order and not chaos ultimately rules the world. God is active in the midst of a broken world to work out HIS good purposes. So the world is a hard place to live, but not normally impossible.

So we must live responsible, sane, stable, and spiritual lives since this is the safest thing to do in a broken world filled with pain. Our actions, words, and attitudes need to reflect a cautious, calculated, and yet hopeful viewpoint. We should prayerfully apply "Common Sense" to every situation and trust in God to use all things together for our good. (Romans 8:28).

A great deal of conflict comes into personal relationships fueled by fear. Anxiety over the future and if we will achieve financial independence by our retirement years can fill our hearts with panic. Fights fueled by worry are one of the main reasons why marriages end. We can also have concerns about many other issues as well.

So what can we do to escape from anxiety? Well the first thing we can do is choose to pray with our spouse or others where our worry could lead to a fight instead of a faithful plan of action. Prayer can calm everyone down. Asking for God's help and wisdom puts the worries we have into a different framework of reference. As the Apostle Paul taught:

"Let your reasonableness be known to everyone. The Lord is at hand; do not be anxious about anything, but in everything by prayer and supplication with thanksgiving let your requests be made known to God. And the peace of God, which surpasses all understanding, will guard your hearts and your minds in Christ Jesus." (Philippians 4:5-7 ESV)

After you pray then sit down and write up a plan. Make a family budget and work to live by it. Or if more time is needed to improve the relationship, then schedule it. Use the brain storming method to fully hear everyone concerning any worries they have. Have weekly meetings aimed at problem solving and write up the ideas and plans that have been developed. What you can do; DO consistently to address, improve, and seek better answers. Be flexible, open, humble, and considerate to what others think.

Frame all of the discussion within a positive framework. Remember life is more than problems. The glass is always half full if you look for it.

"Finally, brothers, whatever is true, whatever is honorable, whatever is just, whatever is pure, whatever is lovely, whatever is commendable, if there is any excellence, if there is anything worthy of praise, think about these things." (Philippians 4:8 ESV)

Fear is the mind killer. If we give in to panic we will start taking radical actions. Radical actions rarely work in the real world. Radical actions create stress and many times break up relationships. Being thoughtful, careful, prudent, calm, positive and kind is the better path and will produce better results in relationships as well.

If you would like to do some additional reading related to this key belief I would recommend.

1. <u>The Mindful Way through Anxiety: Break Free from Chronic Worry and Reclaim Your Life</u> by Susan M. Orsillo PhD, Lizabeth Roemer PhD, Zindel V. Segal PhD

2. The Anxiety Cure by Dr. Archibald D. Hart

3. Telling Yourself the Truth: Find Your Way Out of Depression, Anxiety, Fear, Anger, and Other Common Problems by Applying the Principles of Misbelief Therapy by Marie Chapian and William Backus

The key to this belief is to live a life of faith and common sense aimed at living a sane and stable life while depending on God to use all the pain and problems of our life for our ultimate good. Trust in God's kind sovereign care over our lives will greatly help us to not allow anxiety to destroy our relationships.

Reflective Questions

1. What do you worry the most about? What causes this to be such a source of anxiety for you? On a scale from 1-10 with 1 being the lowest and 10 the highest level of fear and worry, how intense is your worry in this area?

2. What have you found to be the best way for you to handle worry in your life? What keeps this from always working?

3. How has worry and anxiety hurt your relationships with other people?

7. It is better to confront and accept difficulties and responsibilities instead of avoiding them. I accept that I am 100% responsible for what I do, say, and my attitudes. I am assertive and proactive in dealing with life.	7. It is better to avoid difficulties and responsibilities whenever possible. I look to find the "easy way" out of difficult situations and try to get around problems instead of solving them. I blame others for my words, actions, and attitudes.

Relationships are not solved by avoiding difficulties and problems. People deal with conflict and difficulties in one of three ways. They can be aggressive, assertive, or passive aggressive.

An aggressive approach responds to conflict and difficulties by throwing a tantrum. They go to war ready to express anger and be abusive. They take a "skunk" approach hoping that people will back away as they make a "stink" or in some cases they become a "wolf" in which they will attack seeking to do real harm to others to get their way. The aggressive approach is like traditional warfare. It is out in the open and clearly seen.

While in the short run aggressive people might temporary get their way, in the long run this destroys relationships and effectiveness. No one is going to become emotionally intimate with a "skunk" or a "wolf" so it is easy for them to feel abandoned and rejected by others. This feeling many times will only fuel their anger and keep them elevated which deepens their isolation from others.

If you find yourself being a "skunk" or even "wolfish" in conflict take a step back and give yourself some space to gain self-control. Think about the cost it has had on your relationships to act out aggressively and determine if you want to keep paying that price. A careful life inventory of the impact of being a "skunk" or "wolf" on the lives we most care about will normally help us to not choose this approach to dealing with conflict.

A passive aggressive response to conflict is to say "yes" but mean "no". When people are being passive aggressive they will avoid conflict by outwardly going along. They will over promise and under deliver. They take a "turtle" approach in which they go and hide in their shells hoping that the danger will pass.

They will become quiet and isolate themselves. They can use their silence as a weapon in which they hope to hurt others by withdrawing from them. They can also be "termites" or "arsonists" where they will work behind the scenes to undermine a decision they disagreed with and cause great harm. They never do this directly but always in a way where they will not be detected or confronted about what they have done. The passive aggressive approach is like guerrilla warfare. It is hidden and hard to see.

Now the passive aggressive approach may seem to work in the short run since conflict can be avoided. However, one of the problems here is that all "turtles" are living in microwaves. The pressures of the conflicts eventually build up inside of them and their "shells" explode.

These explosions are normally more violent and dangerous than when one runs into a "skunk". In most cases where an emotional elevation becomes lethal it is because a person who was a "turtle" exploded. Years of suppressing anger can lead us to totally losing control and releasing decades of emotion in one desperate action.

In the long run those who choose the passive aggressive approach to handling conflicts cannot build emotional intimacy with others. They will find themselves feeling isolated and alone, which is the only state in which they feel safe. Their desires to be free of conflict leads them to be abandoned and rejected; which creates pain in them, driving them even deeper into their shells.

If you find that you are using passive aggressive tactics when you are in conflict with some people then it is important that you find ways to safely and carefully express your point of view. Silence must not be seen as "safe" but instead as "dangerous" since it is working against the well-being of the relationship itself. I must determine that I will voice my thoughts and not retreat when I see conflict arise. Doing an inventory of what being a passive aggressive has cost my family, friends, and relationships because I failed to share my point of view needs to be carefully done.

The best approach is one that is not aggressive or passive aggressive. It is not to be a wolf, skunk, turtle, or termite. When conflict comes which is always does, the best approach is to be assertive. We see this as the "butterfly" or "dragonfly" approach because it is seen as a dynamic process that moves to maturity.

The assertive approach to conflict is one in which I treat others with love and respect while also treating myself with love and respect. I have learned how to speak the truth in love. When conflict or difficulties arise it is seen as just a normal part of life and the need is to find a solution. The assertive person sees conflict as a process out of which is born a new stage or potential in life.

That is why assertive people are "butterflies" or "dragonflies" who transform conflicts and hardships into a metamorphous aimed at growth. An assertive person will state their own position while respectfully listening to the viewpoint of others.

They are not a "door mat". They know how to set boundaries and can say "no" when they need to do that in the process. Their focus is not in dominating others or in being safe, but instead they seek a solution to the conflict or difficulty. They would be diplomats, ambassadors, and peacemakers. They are not involved in "relationship war" but in the constructive building up of relationships.

Now in the vast majority of relationships it is better to seek to find ways to be assertive. By being assertive I am involved in healthy communication with other people. This develops trust. Others feel respected and loved in the process.

Mistakes are forgiven and overlooked for the goal of finding a solution. People are treated in a merciful way because this process is not about condemnation but healthy resolution of the conflict. Only by people being assertive can they know emotional intimacy, true friendship, and healthy relationships. This is a vital belief for those who would want to succeed in relationships.

For further reading on this subject I would suggest

1. <u>No More Mr. Nice Guy : Saying Goodbye to Doormat Christianity</u> by Stephen Brown

2.   <u>The Assertiveness Workbook: How to Express Your Ideas and Stand Up for Yourself at Work and in Relationships</u> by Randy J. Paterson Ph.D

So to be proactive and assertive is the path that will lead to healthy emotions and relationships. It is an approach that seems less natural to us than being aggressive or defensive; but is the only one that can really establish good relationships with others in the long run.

Reflective Questions

1. Do I have a tendency to handle conflict in a aggressive or passive aggressive manner? What makes it easier to handle problems in this way?

2. What hinders me from being assertive in my relationship with others? How could I become more assertive in conflict?

3. What has caused the most damage to relationships in my life when conflicts have occurred? Have most conflicts been able to be resolved or have they led to bad outcomes?

Eighth key belief needed to have healthy relationships

8. Believe that God has an ultimate purpose for my life and that all my pain has gain.	8. Life is ruled by chaos. There is not purpose or plan. My pain is in vain.

"And we know that for those who love God all things work together for good, for those who are called according to his purpose."
(Romans 8:28 ESV)

"Your eyes saw my unformed substance; in your book were written, every one of them, the days that were formed for me, when as yet there was none of them." (Psalms 139:16 ESV)

Life's but a walking shadow, a poor player
That struts and frets his hour upon the stage
And then is heard no more: it is a tale
Told by an idiot, full of sound and fury,
Signifying nothing. - Macbeth, Shakespeare

We can either believe that our lives are ultimately part of a great and grand plan or simply sound and fury, signifying nothing. The one faith in destiny, legacy, and purpose allows us to endure pain and disappointment in relationships in hope that in the end our sacrifices will mean something. The other leads us to despair and cynicism. We find that we easily exchange relationships hoping perhaps that the next one will end better. This is a basic choice about how we look at life but has huge impact on our attitude and approach to how we relate to people and to ourselves.

I have found that there are five truths that help me to remain focused during times when I am facing difficult times in significant relationships and life in general. My five core truths are:

1. God is good
2. God is great
3. God is full of grace
4. Life has grief in it
5. All my grief will lead ultimately to gain

By stepping back from the problems and struggle that I find myself in and taking a moment to review these five truths I find that I can regain balance within myself to face the difficulties of the day.

What do these five statements mean?

1. God is good. I must ultimately believe that God is good in character. He is the true HERO. God is to be admired because HE is remarkably brave in loving and creating people who can and do rebel against HIM. HE knew that HIS love would cause HIM pain and sacrifice; but HE still decided to love and create. God has freely and consistently understood and practiced the way of VIRTUE for all eternity. HE loves righteousness, purity, and integrity. HE has all wisdom about all things and always acts in accordance with what is wise. HE is fully trustworthy in every way.

2. God is great. Whatever can be done, God can do. HIS power can create universes. HE only needs to speak and it will happen. There is never a situation that is greater than HIS power. God's greatness is only limited by HIS goodness and HIS logic for HE would never choose to compromise HIS character.

3. God is full of grace. God's love is infinite. HE has loved us even when we were HIS enemies and had Messiah Jesus die for our sins and be raised that we might be reconciled to HIS love. God does not give us what we deserve but is patient with us and gives us time to repent. Paul the Apostle summarizes it well in these words.

"And you were dead in the trespasses and sins in which you once walked, following the course of this world, following the prince of the power of the air, the spirit that is now at work in the sons of disobedience-- among whom we all once lived in the passions of our flesh, carrying out the desires of the body and the mind, and were by nature children of wrath, like the rest of mankind."

"But God, being rich in mercy, because of the great love with which he loved us, even when we were dead in our trespasses, made us alive together with Christ--by grace you have been saved-- and raised us up with him and seated us with him in the heavenly places in Christ Jesus, so that in the coming ages he might show the immeasurable riches of his grace in kindness toward us in Christ Jesus. For by grace you have been saved through faith. And this is not your own doing; it is the gift of God, not a result of works, so that no one may boast." (Ephesians 2:1-9 ESV)

There is hope for us even when we make mistakes because God has mercy, compassion, pity, and grace upon us. God is the God of second chances.

4.   Life has grief in it. Because we left the paradise of God in rebellion and pride we now live "East of Eden". The world we live in is filled with struggle and pain. We find it hard to love and be loved. We suffer physically, emotionally, and spiritually. There is much sorrow in this life and no one is exempt from losing loved ones and seeing our dreams go unfulfilled. I must not be surprised by painful events but come to expect them as just part of life.

5.   All my grief will ultimately lead to gain. No one can choose a life free of grief and pain. But we can choose how we look at that grief. Either we see it as "sound and fury" signifying nothing or we look at it as part of a larger tapestry which God is weaving based on a design that only HIS wisdom can fully discern. Right now we see only the back of the tapestry which many times seems only like a tangle of aimless yarn. But once we see the face of it we will see that every strand of pain and struggle was needed in order to bring about the wonder and awe of the final work of art which God is making. None of my pain will be without gain in the end. Paul the Apostle again helps us understand this truth when he writes:

"And we know that for those who love God all things work together for good, for those who are called according to his purpose. For those whom he foreknew he also predestined to be conformed to the image of his Son, in order that he might be the firstborn among many brothers. And those whom he predestined he also called, and those whom he called he also justified, and those whom he justified he also glorified. What then shall we say to these things? If God is for us, who can be against us? He who did not spare his own Son but gave him up for us all, how will he not also with him graciously give us all things? Who shall bring any charge against God's elect? It is God who justifies.

Who is to condemn? Christ Jesus is the one who died--more than that, who was raised--who is at the right hand of God, who indeed is interceding for us. Who shall separate us from the love of Christ? Shall tribulation, or distress, or persecution, or famine, or nakedness, or danger, or sword? As it is written, "For your sake we are being killed all the day long; we are regarded as sheep to be slaughtered." No, in all these things we are more than conquerors through him who loved us. For I am sure that neither death nor life, nor angels nor rulers, nor things present nor things to come, nor powers, nor height nor depth, nor anything else in all creation, will be able to separate us from the love of God in Christ Jesus our Lord." (Romans 8:28-39 ESV)

Now the choice is ours. Either we will choose to be cynical and despairing or believe in the grand designer despite the struggle and hardship of life. People choose both things. But the results are radically different.

Can we choose? Is it possible when relationships are filled with hatred and abuse for us to really see God's plan in the midst of it all? Is it possible for people to hold on to hope when their lives are filled with pain?

Victor Frankl wrote a book, <u>Man's Search for Meaning</u> after he survived the concentration camps of Nazism during World War II. He assures us that we can make such a choice even under the darkest of circumstances.

"We can answer these questions from experience as well as on principle. The experiences of camp life show that man does have a choice of action. There were enough examples, often of a heroic nature, which proved that apathy could be overcome, irritability suppressed. Man can preserve a vestige of spiritual freedom, of independence of mind, even in such terrible conditions of psychic and physical stress.

We who lived, in concentration camps can remember the men who walked through the huts comforting others, giving away their last piece of bread. They may have been few in number, but they offer sufficient proof that everything can be taken from a man but one thing: the last of the human freedoms — to choose one's attitude in any given set of circumstances, to choose one's own way."

We can choose our way. We can give into despair, frustration, cynicism, doubt, anger, and depression. That is really easy. Or we can face the grief of this life with confidence that God will work it for good. This allows us to have hope, patience, vision, faith, gentleness, and perseverance.

All of this is based on the attitude we choose to have. It is all based on the narratives that we allow to dominate our minds which then create in us either noble feelings of faith or fearful attitudes of greed and vice.

For those who would like to read some books that would help deepen this idea I would recommend.

1. <u>When God & Grief Meet: True Stories of Comfort and Courage</u> by Lynn Eib

2. <u>When God Doesn't Make Sense</u> by James C. Dobson

3. <u>The Problem of Pain</u> by C.S. Lewis

3. <u>A Grief Observed</u> by C. S. Lewis

It is vital that we come to trust in a plan behind all the events of our lives. Only when we have this perspective will we be able to demonstrate patience and compassion as we deal with hurtful events that occur in our lives and our relationships. This gives us a foundation upon which we can strive to act in a sane, stable, and spiritual way even when no one around us is choosing to act in such a way.

Such an attitude allows us to provide sanity and stability to those around us. We become a positive influence in every relationship. Instead of becoming part of the problem we are part of the solution during every crisis.

Reflective Questions

1. What makes you doubt that God has a good plan for your life? What could you do to overcome these doubts?

2. What advantages would it have in your life for you to believe the "five key truths" which have been suggested?

3. What do you normally say to yourself when bad things happen in a relationship? Is your self talk true or false? How could you change it?

Ninth key belief needed to have sane relationships

9. Believe that God uses broken people. I live by God's grace alone which is found in Messiah Jesus. I accept myself as the imperfect, limited, and fallible child of God. It is direction not perfection that matters. It is part of life to grow, learn, and change. This is a normal part of life. I can learn from the mistakes I made in the past. If I confess my sins to God I will be forgiven and can move forward in life.	9. Good things can only come to me when I have been perfect. I believe I will succeed if I am competent, intelligent, and super achieving in all I do. It is perfection that counts not direction. I cannot admit my mistakes because that would mean I am wrong. My self esteem and self acceptance is based on me never being wrong. I never feel forgiven over anything I have done wrong and live in denial, shame and guilt

It is not perfection but direction that matters. If we demand perfection or nothing we will always get nothing. Rejecting thinking in black and white categories is vital to having healthy relationships. We must look at life in "grey" and not in "black and white".

Now this does not mean we do not strive to do better. It is vital that we continue daily to strive to do better, every day. This means we know that our best efforts are not perfect.

Because we know that God accepts us not on the basis of our deeds but due to HIS grace alone we can see that our efforts please our heavenly FATHER even when they are less than perfect.

Our self esteem and self love must not be based on our performance but on God's unconditional love and grace. We need to know that God has made us "great" in that we reflect HIS image and we need to value ourselves because it took the suffering of Christ Jesus on the cross to purchase our pardon. It is what we are, not what we do that matters to God and should matter to us. God uses us in our imperfection for the good of others. HE allows our imperfect efforts to work and bring good to many. God uses broken sticks to accomplish HIS will on earth.

We must also recognize that others are valuable to God for the same reasons. We need to give unconditional love and respect to others. Each person in our lives can be used by God to help us grow in various ways. We need to accept them with their vices and virtues.

Only when we stop expecting perfection from people will we be able to have healthy relationships with them. In this way we will not idolize the person when the demonstrate their virtue or demonize them when a vice gets the best of them. We will expect that at various times people will demonstrate being "saints" and at other times reveal themselves as "sinners". We will accept the reality that "all have sinned and come short of the glory of God."

Yet, God uses less than perfect people all the time. Moses was a murderer but was used by God to lead the Exodus. Paul was a persecutor of the church but became a great church planter. Not one person in the Bible that God uses was without significant faults.

The Trap of Perfectionism

We feel a lot of anxiety because we believe that we have to be perfect or we will fail. When people suffer from perfectionism they set unrealistically high goals for their character and competence. Regardless of how hard they work they feel that they have to work more. Regardless of how much they accomplish they feel they have to accomplish more. They are driven and stressful at their best moments. At their worst moments they are feeling depressed and defeated.

Perfectionists also believe that anything that others do that hurts them could have been avoided if only they had done better. If they had been a better spouse then the other person would not abuse them. If they had been a better parent their children would make better choices. Every problem in every relationship is for the perfectionist evidence of their failure. This gives them a sense of being in control of everything in their life; but the cost of this is self condemnation and unrealistic guilt.

Perfectionism can also be an outward attitude. We can make our love and acceptance of others conditional upon their performance. Eventually every person fails and so all our relationships are very fragile. We end up condemning everyone in our lives. People don't like to be condemned and so normally will abandon or reject those who are telling them that they are falling short of expectations. Perfectionist will many times say "no one can be trusted" because everyone they know has failed them and abandoned them. What the perfectionist cannot see is that this is because of a "script" in their minds that demands perfection or nothing.

How can we overcome perfectionism?

- You have to realize you are worthy of love and respect by just being you, not what you accomplish or achieve in life.
- Stop the negative thoughts of you should or you must, or you have to; perform or no one will love you.
- Remember it is direction not perfection that counts?
- Concentrate on all the positives instead of the negatives.
- Be honest and don't set your goals too high.

Becoming less of a perfectionist can greatly help your relationships with others and with your acceptance of yourself. It also can give you hope of leaving a godly legacy in this world since God uses imperfect people to accomplish his will on earth. If we change how we view the world at this very basic level it can radically change our lives.

For those who would like to read more on this subject let me recommend.

1. <u>Too Perfect: When Being in Control Gets Out of Control</u> by Jeannette Dewyze and Allan Mallinger

2. <u>When Your Best Isn't Good Enough: The Secret of Measuring Up</u> Dr. Kevin Leman

Only by reducing our perfectionism both for ourselves and others can we hope to have sane, stable, and spiritual relationships with others and peace in our own heart.

The key to answering perfectionism is the gospel. How can God accept and use imperfect people? It is because HE gives us grace and not pure justice. God has had the Messiah Jesus die for us so that we cannot be separated from HIS love and be used by HIM to bring great good into the world. Mercy opens up new doors of opportunity and being at peace with people.

Reflective Questions

1. How has perfectionism impacted my life? Do I know any perfectionists?

2. When I look at my life do I focus on the glass "half full" and recognize what I have been able to do or do I focus on the glass "half empty" feeling defeated and depressed?

Tenth key belief needed to have sane relationships

10. I do not control other people or circumstances at all. They are outside my control and yet I can enjoy life.	10. I can only be happy when the circumstances and people in my life are under my control.

When we believe that we can control other people we will abuse other people. This abuse can be physical, emotional, or spiritual. Our passion for controlling others is that we believe that our happiness depends on them doing certain things. We can also believe that their happiness depends on us controlling them since we don't trust the decisions they make. Our desire to have power and control over other people can be motivated due to a strong conviction that we know what is best for them. We can only feel secure when we are in control of everyone in our lives.

Part of this is our belief that if we have the right "formula" then we can determine the circumstances of our life. We believe that we can exercise a type of "mind over matter" by being positive and focused. Health, wealth, happy children, an adoring spouse, an appreciative employer, and every type of prosperity can be ours if only we "play our cards" right. We believe that there are a set of "life rules" which if we follow have to then produce all we want. When we strive to have power and control over all aspects of our lives by carefully following these "life rules" this normally ends up making us frustrated and angry when our "ideal life" does not materialize. We become bitter not better through this process.

While we would like to have people and events treat us well, this is outside of our control. People can choose to return evil for good. Circumstances will at times be painful and not be what we would want. Sometimes I will keep all of the "rules of life" and yet face hardship while someone else will break all the "rules of life" and have everything I want. It will not seem fair. We will normally not notice how many times we break the "rules of life" and not suffer bad consequences. The bottom line is this. We have influence but no control over other people and circumstances. At most we can learn to have self-control and this is not easy.

However, no circumstance or even the evil decision of another person, can keep me from God's love or plan. HE is at work in my life and therefore I can take joy in my life. All my pain will be used in the end to develop in me a Christ like character and produce ultimate good. There is gain in my pain.

The way to enjoy life is to embrace what I have today as God's will for me today instead of wanting some other state of things that only exists in my mind. The worst enemy of the real is the ideal. Once I have embraced my current state then I can begin to look for ways to make lemonade out of lemons.

We think about what the "ideal" spouse would be like and then find ourselves unhappy with our real spouse. Our minds start constructing what we would like as the "ideal" job and we work less diligently at our real job. Only when we embrace the "real" can we adapt to it. Only when we accept the "real" can we find joy in our circumstances. It is only at this point that we can have peace in our circumstances instead of hoping for a new set of circumstances which will make us happy.

Now some circumstances give us more pleasure than other circumstances. Some situations are very painful. But pleasure is not happiness or joy. Pleasure, when gained through moral means is good. When we gain pleasure through immoral means it is not good. Pleasure is a fleeting experience that cannot be maintained. When experienced within God's will is a wonderful gift of God. When experienced by rebelling against God's will it becomes a temptation to do wrong.

True happiness comes from living a sane, stable, and spiritual life day by day and moment by moment. Sane relationships develop between people who are both striving to be sane, stable, and spiritual in their words, actions, and attitudes. The more sanity, stability, and spirituality I have and the more sanity, stability, and spirituality the other people in my life have; then we experience healthy, happy, and sane relationships with each other. So while I like pleasure, it is true mature happiness that I must seek if I hope to succeed in having sane and healthy relationships with others.

Only when we recognize that our only control is over ourselves will we not be abusive to others. The desire to have power and control of others is a basic motivation in human relationships. Only by respecting others boundaries and letting them disagree with us in an agreeable manner, can I hope to have long lasting and mutually beneficial relationships.

What this means is that I focus on doing God's will in my life and recognize that they must seek God's will for their lives. I can encourage them and strive to influence them to seek and do God's will. But, I do not have the power or the responsibility to make them do the "right thing" and I become abusive when I try to force them to do the "right thing."

Overcoming our desire to have power and control

The first thing that we need to recognize is that gaining power and control over a person by being abusive physically, emotionally, or spiritually can never lead to emotional intimacy. The more we strive to control our spouse, our children, or our employees the more they will put up walls to keep us out of their lives. People respond to others attempting to control them by becoming defensive and withdrawn. They can also choose to become hurtful and abusive in response to our threats, anger, and efforts to manipulate them to do our will. People are not emotionally intimate with people who they see as a danger to them.

The next thing we must come to see is that people do not trust others who try to have power and control over them. We see efforts to control us not as being in our best interest but rather as the "controller" attempting to manipulate us for their own good and comfort. Adults feel they are being treated as children when other adults try to control them. If we want to have relationships of mutual respect then we cannot be attempting to have power and control over other people.

The last thing is that we have to recognize that if our aim is to know the other person this means knowing how they differ with us on significant issues. Adults have the right to disagree. We need to not desire for every person in our life to be simply a "clone" of our attitudes and desires. We need to value the fact that the other people in our lives have different personalities than we do and different perspectives. Out of this dynamic interaction of differences great things can come if we decide to disagree in an agreeable manner. Great creativity is born out of conflict when this encounter is managed by love and respect for each other.

Power and control cannot lead to emotional intimacy, trust, or honest communication. It has no promise of fixing any relationship in our lives. We must begin to doubt our power and control tactics on a regular basis and this can transform our lives.

Signs of Power and Control

Our ministry deals with many people who struggle with power and control issues. Here are some of the signs that power and control have entered into a relationship.

1. Using gender privilege. This is where it is implied that being "male" or being "female" comes with a built in superiority. When we are in relationship with someone of the opposite gender we imply that because of being "male" or "female" we are smarter, more mature, or stronger. Because of our "gender" we should be allowed to make all the big decisions in the relationship. There will be a lot of "gender truth jokes" such as

"Women are always emotional"

"All men are boys"

"It must be that time of month again"

"Don't imagine you can change a man - unless he's in diapers."

"Never let your man's mind wander - it's too little to be left out alone."

"Did you hear they finally made a device that makes cars run 95% quieter? Yeah, it fits right over her mouth."

This type of abusive humor communicates a lack of respect towards those of the other gender and attempts to put the other person "in their place" which should be one of not being treated as an equal adult.

2. Minimizing, denying and blaming the other person for hurtful words and actions which have been done to intimidate them into doing what is desired. This can cause the other person to feel like they are "crazy" and they can begin to doubt themselves. If they can be made to feel guilty, then this may make them more likely to comply

with what we want. This is a classic tactic is striving to have power and control over others.

3. Using isolation from other people to make the person overly dependent is a common power and control tactic. Instead of the relationship being one of several, every effort is made to cut off other family and friends from the person and make them feel guilty for spending time with anyone else. This can lead to a "co-dependent relationship where the "controller" gets to play a parent role over the other adult.

4. Using emotional and verbal abuse is a common tactic in attempting to control others. When we do things that will hurt the feelings of another person if they do not do what we want then this is an effort to control them. Calling people names, yelling, attacking their character, and swearing are all means of intimidating people into complying with what we want. Tantrums can influence people to do whatever they need to do to quiet the situation down. This can be used by people to try to get their way.

5. Using intimidation by implying that if they do not obey then they will suffer for it physically is a power and control tactic.   When actions or words have the goal of creating fear, feelings of inadequacy, or a sense of peril then they are intimidating. Such power and control tactics can be very subtle like "a look" or very aggressive such as physically destroying a favorite possession to demonstrate the power of the person who wants to be in control.

6. Using coercion and threats is a common tactic when people strive to have power and control over other people. Here there is a very formal and clear verbal formula used. If you don't do what I want then I will cause you a huge amount of pain, embarrassment, and hardship. Obey me or face destruction. This is a common tactic in attempting to gain power and control over others.

7. Using economic abuse is a factor in many relationships where one person has control of all the finances. When the other adult attempts to communicate their point of view they are minimized because of their lack of financial strength in the relationship. Normally the person who is stronger in such relationships will strive to make sure the other person remains dependent on them financially.

8. Using children as pawns in a chess game. If a spouse thinks or feels differently; then this is said to in some way be harmful to the children. For the spouse to disagree is for them to not love their children or care for their wellbeing. Comments like this are not really about the children, they are just being used to gain power and control over the other parent.

9. Sexual abuse comes when the purpose of the sex is to prove power and dominance instead of mutually expressing love in marriage. When sex is connected to anger then it can become abusive and aimed at putting someone in their place. Denying sexuality until the other person does what we want is another type of sexual abuse. Attempting to get the other person to do things they don't want to do sexually is also an attempt to gain a sense of power and control over them. This type of abuse deeply damages marriages and relationships.

10. Spiritual abuse is when we threaten them with God's judgment if they don't do what we want. We can also attempt to bring in other "religious people" who agree with us in order to try to make them feel guilty over not doing what we want to do. Religion and God are simply tools here to gain dominance and control over the other person.

Most of us have a great desire to gain control over other people. We will use many of the tactics listed above to do this. Only when we see that all such actions weaken the trust, security, and true communication in a relationship will we be able to begin to stop these destructive behaviors.

For those who would want to read more on this topic I would recommend;

1. <u>The Power of Losing Control</u> by Joe Caruso

2. <u>Compelled to Control: Recovering Intimacy in Broken Relationships</u> by J. Keith Miller

3. <u>Angry Men and the Women Who Love Them: Breaking the Cycle of Physical and Emotional Abuse</u> by Paul Hegstrom

Only when we deeply believe that we have no control of others can we treat them with the respect and dignity they deserve. We will become "safe" people in their lives. This also allows us to enjoy imperfect people and frees us from the need to judge, condemn, and manipulate others in order to enjoy life. Seeing God work through imperfection deepens our trust in God's ability to work. With less stress in our lives we can begin to enjoy life as it really is and not make our happiness dependent on people living "ideally". By adapting to the "real" world we can live a sane, stable, and spiritual life with sane, stable, and spiritual relationships.

Reflective Questions

1. What makes it scary to admit that I have no control over other people or the circumstances in my life?

2. How have I hurt others because I have attempted to have power and control over people?

3. What steps could you take to see God working in imperfect people and enjoy the life you have more than you do?

Eleventh key belief needed to have healthy relationships

11. The goal of my life is to fulfill my godly passions, use my God given abilities, and take advantage of my God given opportunities to live a life that glorifies God.	11. The goal of my life is to have enough resources to do nothing everyday and be free of responsibilities.

Everyone has a purpose. God has given us what we need to live a life that will give HIM glory. Our life is a gift from God. We are responsible to manage well this gift well.

This also means that every person in my life is a person placed there by God. This includes my friends and my enemies. My response and reaction to them is how God plans to direct my life and develop my character. I can choose to see every relationship as not an accident but as part of God working in my life even when the relationship is difficult.

We need to see our lives as a great quest and not a process of attempting to "retire" so we can do nothing all day. People without purpose do not prosper. Relationships which share a common purpose are stronger than when there is no shared vision in the relationship.

Many people have created an "ideal" retirement as a time to stop working. But research shows that people who take on full- or part-time jobs after retirement have better health. The key to a good retirement is not to retire.

William Safire the political writer said the following about retirement.

"But retraining and fresh stimulation are what all of us should require in the last of life, for which the first was made... We can quit a job, but we quit fresh involvement at our mental peril... When you're through changing, learning, working, to stay involved-only then are you through."

In an article in the New York Times entitled "For a Healthy Retirement, Keep Working" by Tara Parker supports this point of view. Researchers from the University of Maryland found that people who kept working after retirement had fewer major diseases or disabilities than those who quit work.

According to the study printed in the Journal of Occupational Health Psychology the best way to retire is not to retire. Retirees benefited whether the work was a full- or part-time job, self-employment, volunteer work or temporary. Using our abilities, expressing our passion, feeling we are making a positive contribution, and having a purpose to get up in the morning helps us to live and prosper. It also allows us to relate to others in a healthier and saner way.

Doctors have long believed that staying active during the older years is associated with better health. But the question is whether working keeps older people healthy, or whether the people who continue working are able to do so because they were healthier to start with. This was hard to know.

But the new research controlled for health before retirement and found that post-retirement work had a distinct effect on health. Remarkably, the hours a person worked didn't matter, showing that both part-time and full-time employments are advantageous after retirement. People live better when they believe that life has purpose.

While working after retirement is good for you, the data also suggest that retirees should take a job that they have a real passion to do. Among those who kept working, the retirees who found work related to their previous careers had the best mental outlook on life. We have less stress and more joy when we feel our work matters and is leaving a legacy to the next generation.

Couples without vision have a tendency to fall into complaining about everything to their spouse and are normally do not hesitate to command them to do things they want. Conversations stop being joint efforts to solve some joint problems but rather hostile encounters that often lead to ugly words and actions. Arguments become regular parts of the conversation. If I don't have a purpose then it is easy to fall into my purpose being to gain control of my spouse.

Couples who continue working feel like "partners" with their spouses. These relationships normally do better than if people just retire to do nothing. There is a friendship and bonding that takes place as we work on joint projects together. This helps us to keep focus in our relationships.

Now this impacts us before we reach the age of "retirement" because it impacts how we are living today. If our aim is to live a full life with a sense of destiny and purpose then we are not "idealizing" a future where we do nothing. When the "ideal" is escaping from responsibility then we become less responsible.

So we should not be thinking about "retiring" but about using our abilities and passions up to the day we die. By having a vision of a life of service we will handle life and relationships better. Our focus should not be seeking to "succeed" by stopping all useful activity but rather to be live purpose driven lives.

For those wanting to read more on this belief; I would recommend:

1. <u>The Purpose Driven Life: What on Earth Am I Here For?</u> By Rick Warren

2. <u>Fully Human, Fully Alive: A New Life Through a New Vision</u> by John Powell

This is part of our life "narrative" because it is how we are imagining the final chapter of our "life book". Our energy, direction, and decision making will be influenced by our desire to finish well. We will do more to preserve and improve our relationships if we see them as part of God's calling and plan for our lives. So how we imagine our future can greatly impact our present

Reflective questions

1. What abilities do I have to use?

2. What do I care about? What is my passion?

3. What opportunities do my relationships make possible? What doors has God opened in my life?

Twelfth key belief needed to have healthy relationships

12. The gospel of Messiah Jesus teaches us that grace, mercy, and tenderness must be at the core of all we do instead of self-righteousness, condemnation, and harshness. We are longsuffering, patient, and forgiving towards those who have hurt us.	12. We judge others by our moral law and condemn them for their failures. We see ourselves as living right and feel angry towards those who are not living right. We are bitter towards those who have hurt us.

"Let no corrupting talk come out of your mouths, but only such as is good for building up, as fits the occasion, that it may give grace to those who hear. And do not grieve the Holy Spirit of God, by whom you were sealed for the day of redemption. Let all bitterness and wrath and anger and clamor and slander be put away from you, along with all malice. Be kind to one another, tenderhearted, forgiving one another, as God in Christ forgave you." (Ephesians 4:29-32 ESV)

The only thing that can reconcile broken relationships is grace, mercy, and compassion. Self righteousness and a focus on fairness will always lead relationships to condemnation, rejection, and death. Only as we see that God has had mercy on us in the death of the Messiah Jesus can we attempt to imitate that grace in how we treat others.

How can we do this? One way is to actually practice a Christian version of the twelve step program in our relationships. The twelve steps of A.A find their roots in an ancient practice of living out the gospel of grace.

12 Steps Towards Reconciliation Of Relationships

Step 1 - I admit that I am powerless over the wounds of my life and my relationships- that my life and my relationships have become unmanageable because of my sin, for which I am 100% responsible.

Step 2 - Come to believe that the Lord Jesus the Messiah has paid for my sins and has been resurrected with all power. I need to believe that the Lord Jesus Christ can restore me to sanity, stability, and spirituality. He can bring healing to the relationships that I have damaged by how I have handled things.

Step 3 - Make a decision to turn my life and my relationships over to the care of the Lord Jesus the Messiah as revealed in the Bible

Step 4 - Make a searching and fearless moral inventory of what I have done to hurt the people in my relationships. On the Day of Judgment what will Lord Jesus the Messiah speak to me about concerning my hurtful actions towards others in my life?   Write out this inventory before the face of God.

Step 5 - Admit to God, to myself and to those I have hurt the exact nature of my wrongs, fully accepting 100% responsibility for my words, actions, and attitudes. In no way will I imply or blame others for my words, actions, and attitudes.

Step 6 – Become ready to stop those patterns of words, actions, and attitudes that harm my relationships. I will seek to change my life commandments, habits, and beliefs that create hurtful words, actions, and attitudes. I will seek new skills and new beliefs that will lead to healthier relationships.

Step 7 - Humbly ask God to remove these hurtful patterns from my life in sustained and repeated prayer and the use of spiritual disciplines. Look for methods that will allow me to be effective in my repentance.

Step 8 – Be willing to make amends to others where I can. I will be willing to walk the extra mile with them and seek to show by positive actions my desire to rebuild trust.

Step 9 – To actually make amends to others wherever possible and develop new patterns of life which demonstrate on a regular basis my new commitment to a healthy relationship.

Step 10 – I will continue to take personal inventory of my actions in the relationships of my life and when I say harmful words, do harmful actions, or develop hurtful attitudes, will confess these and seek to change this behavior quickly.

Step 11 – I will seek through prayer and meditation to improve my conscious contact with my Lord Jesus the Messiah, praying for knowledge of God's will for my relationships and the power to carry that out will.

Step 12 - Having had a spiritual awakening as the result of these steps and seeing the restoration of my relationships, I will share these steps with others that are struggling in the hope that their relationships may also be restored.

Can any of us doubt that any person who consistently applied this process to the relationships they have in their lives would see a significant healing take place in the relationships they have in their lives. It is not easy to follow these 12 steps consistently. But the reality is that the more we would do such things in our lives the more sane our relationships would be.

For those seeking to deepen their knowledge of how to make this work in their lives I would recommend the following books:

1. A Hunger for Healing: The Twelve Steps as a Classic Model for Christian Spiritual Growth by J. Keith Miller

2. The Life Recovery Workbook: A Biblical Guide through the Twelve Steps by Stephen Arterburn

3. True Spirituality by Francis A. Schaeffer

To have good relationships we must be sane, stable, and spiritual. The healthier our soul is before God the more effective we will be in showing love and compassion towards others. Only by having the power of the gospel active in our lives will we find effective ways to avoid becoming bitter and instead become better, day by day. The sane live by faith.

Reflective Questions

1. If I did not believe in the gospel of Christ Jesus how would this impact the relationships I have with others?

2. When was the last time I gave someone a sincere apology? Is it easy or hard for me to admit that I have done wrong?

3. List all the virtues of the most important people in your life. Review their best traits several times during the day. Does this help you feel differently towards them?

This chapter has focused on the fact that our relationships are sane or insane due to the core beliefs that dominate our lives.

We have looked at twelve key beliefs and how they can help create sane relationships.   Write out in your own words the twelve healthy beliefs here:

As your review this list of beliefs which ones do you have to work to really adopt and accept?

What steps will you take to review and remind yourself of the key beliefs that you most have to change?

 How could the right beliefs help you to live effectively?

How are unhealthy beliefs hindering your life today?

Ultimately, what we believe will control everything else in our lives.

Chapter Four -r <u>The Blueprint for Sane Relationships</u>

Sane human relationships must have three elements if they are to be healthy. These three elements are commitment, communication, and craze. If these three elements become weaker the relationship becomes weaker. If these three elements become stronger then the relationship becomes stronger. These three elements provide a blue print to a successful and sane relationship.

Commitment – This will vary from relationship to relationship. A relationship without commitment is really not a relationship at all. Commitment is a vital ingredient to any relationship. Commitment means we keep our promises. We "under promise" and "over deliver" in any relationship we want to work.

In marriage the commitment is "till death do we part". This is also true in our parenting relationships. This means that our aim is to always love our spouse and children unconditionally and that we will always be "in relationship" with them up to the day they die. Now sometimes in marriages there is infidelity and other extreme abuse that breaks up the marriage. But in principle we are bonded together, "for better, for worse, in riches and in poverty, and in sickness and in health."

Circumstances do not destroy our commitment. To be committed to another person means that we are devoted to them, will give them time and energy to the relationship, and will be loyal to them in our role as spouse or parent. Commitment means we will stick with the relationship in both good and bad times.

In our friendships commitment is the loyalty we have to be there for the other person regardless of how they mess up. Under what circumstances would we abandon our friendship? There is a mutual desire to seek win/win solutions in the relationship of friends. This is also a commitment to try to make the relationship work. Loyalty to our friends is normally not as absolute as to our family. The promises given are less. The greater our commitment, then the stronger the friendship is in our lives.

In our business life we find that we can be committed to our company, our employees, and our customers. Our business life can become complicated because commitment to one group of people may put us in conflict with others. We have to prioritize our commitments and define carefully our role to avoid conflicting loyalties. We will also have to balance our commitment to our work with the commitment we need to have for our family.

Our society fears commitment at every level. We don't want to give promises about what we will do tomorrow. Our fear is that a promise might limit our happiness because some greater opportunity might arise. Because of this lack of commitment in human relationships we see an increase in stress and less trust of people. Relationships are very fragile where loyalty is low.

Commitment is reflected in public vows, contracts, shaking hands on an issue, and promises exchanged. As people begin to avoid these cultural expressions of commitment it can reflect a desire to avoid being faithful and loyal to someone else. When a culture makes light of commitment we will see a decline in the quality of the relationships enjoyed by that culture.

Our society has now accepted living together before marriage as a normal part of life. The original idea of this was that by living together this would allow people to get to know each other better and reduce the chance of divorce. This is the belief of most Americans today according to Gallup.

However, the statistics seem to indicate that those that live together actually have a higher risk of divorce then couples that don't live together. Some of the statistics put those who live together as having as high as an 80% greater chance of divorce while others report only a 50% increased rate of divorce. There is no evidence that living together makes divorce less likely. A lack of commitment does not make life more stable.

Just do a search on the internet on "living together and divorce" and see what you find. There is little to encourage the idea that living together increases commitment or makes divorce less likely. In fact, the opposite is reality, but the illusion that we are safer by living together before marriage persists. It appears that those who live together also have less of a commitment to marriage to begin with and therefore a higher divorce rate is to be expected.

So we have to think through and become aware of what we feel about commitment. We have to make a decision to give our love and promises to others. We have to decide to have them in our lives and care about them. The people we give our commitments to will be imperfect and flawed. They will sometimes betray us. What makes commitment hard is that it is given to imperfect people who will fail us. Yet, commitment is a vital key to relationships. Without mutual commitment then relationships have no foundation.

Communication - This is where we are telling each other our "life story". This is also our ability to resolve conflicts together. We seek here to understand the other person and to be understood by them.

Communication has two aspects to it. One is a maintenance level of communication that keeps people feeling in touch. This is where we share "our story" with another person in some type of narrative. We share the good things that have happened, the struggles and bad things we have endured, the ugly things that at times we have done which we are not proud of, and the dreams we have for our lives in the future. The more deeply we share stories which reflect the good, the bad, the ugly, and our dreams the more people will feel they know us.   Trust is developed many times because of us hearing the "life story" of the other person.

When people share their good, bad, ugly, and dreams with us in response to us sharing our story with them, this leads to emotional intimacy. We all seek to be heard. When others share their story with us we normally feel honored.   Typically the people who are in our inner circle will be those we share our life story with at least one hour a week.

This is a great exercise for married couples to use in their relationships. Committing thirty minutes a day to share our stories to our spouses can create the emotional intimacy we all desire. If we share the good, the bad, our ugly, and our dreams with our spouses over a ninety day period there can be a real opening up of our emotions to each other.

Familiarity can bred contempt. Sometimes those we are the closest to we want to control. We then begin to complain, nag, and command. We don't share our stories. Our efforts get aimed at getting those closest to us to change. It seems that the only way to do this is to win a battle of the wills with those who are closest to us. So the main communication becomes one of argument and manipulation. This is the danger of power and control.

To maintain good communication with others we need "story telling" time. The people who share their lives with co-workers become the center of the social life at work. Those who listen to others with a sympathetic ear gain even more influence. Most people don't feel heard and feel greatly honored when someone listens to them. The same is true in families, friendships, lovers, and spouses. It is important that we understand how significant it is when we share our "stories" with other people and actively listen to their stories. This is a key to developing strong and sane relationships.

The second type of communication that is needed in a healthy relationship is that designed to handle the "crisis" moments when conflict is felt. Conflict is when people who have a relationship disagree on vision, values, or strategy. We find that that we deeply disagree on what needs to be done or how it is to be done. Most people do not know how to resolve conflicts in a healthy manner.

When conflict arises most people only know "argument" as the tool to handle it. In argument our effort is to either cause the other person so much pain that they will just let us do what we want to do or abuse the other person so much that they will agree with us just to end being subject to our abuse. We can hurt them more than they can hurt us. When I choose to argue my goal is to gain power and control over the other person.

Arguments can use many different tactics. We can get loud to intimidate, threaten to cause fear, express anger to put force behind our words, verbally abuse to make the other person feel weak, or withdraw to manipulate the other due to the anxiety caused by rejection and abandonment. Everyone knows how to argue. Some do it better than others.

The problem is that argument at best creates a fragile and false resolution to the conflict. One person may feel forced to agree today to what has been set forth as the answer to the conflict but will most likely try to get out of the agreement when they think they can. This will resurrect the issue and the fight. Argument seems to set the stage for recycling conflicts over and over again.

In addition the relationship itself is normally damaged by arguments. As we hurt each other by our words, actions, and attitudes the trust and admiration we had for the other person begins to wither. We begin putting up "walls" around us to keep from getting hurt.

Relationships that have a history of arguments become distant, cold, and detached. So arguments do not lead to emotional intimacy, trust, or mutual admiration.

So what can we do when conflicts arise? There is a process that requires first of all that we "stop" and keep the conflict from falling into an argument. Then the people with the conflict need to systematically seek to establish a true "peace" about the conflict.

The hardest thing to do is to "STOP" the argument before we become so elevated and emotional that we are just working out of our emotional part of our brain instead of our most reasonable selves. We must develop a true fear of using abusive arguments as a method of resolving conflicts. This can be done by making a list of the emotional, physical, and financial cost of abusive arguments in our lives. We need to review this list daily to give us good reasons to stop the process that leads to an angry argument before it is too late.

So how can we STOP getting into arguments when there are conflicts? The first thing we need to remember is that stopping is not denying the conflict or refusing to find resolution. It is in fact just setting the stage for a sane, healthy and true resolution to the problem. The aim is not to avoid the conflict but to avoid abuse. Our goal is to have good communication not no communication.

When I become aware that I am beginning to become elevated over a conflict or that the other person is becoming elevated, I need to stop. I need to say; "I need some time to think about this issue and I want us to find a real answer to this issue. Give me about a half hour to think and pray about this and then let us get back together again." At this point see if the other person can meet with you in a half hour and if not set a definite time to continue the conversation. The other person may say; "Why can't we do this now?". Tell them that because they are important to you and the issue is important to you that you want to be ready to hear what they say objectively. Just say; "I don't want us just to have an argument over this issue; I want us to find an answer."

So the first things to do are just STOP and take a breath.

The second thing to do is THINK.

Once you have stopped the process of falling into argument you now can prepare yourself for the peace process. Answer the following questions for yourself and even write out your answers to clarify your thinking and feelings about what is happening.

First Question: What is this conflict about? What is the issue at hand? It is objective or subjective? Is it about how something should be done or what should be done? Is this because of a conflict of values or just practically what will work? Has this conflict come up before in this relationship? What has been done in the past to resolve it? What has kept this issue from being resolved? How do I think the other person views this conflict? How is their perspective different than mine?

Second Question: How do I feel about this conflict? Am I angry? Am I afraid? Am I frustrated? Do I feel guilt? Is there shame over this issue? Is this an embarrassing issue? Am I confused? Am I hopeless over this issue? Am I determined to get my way regardless of the cost? What are my emotions about this issue?

Third Question: What would be an acceptable answer to this conflict? What do I believe would be a good answer for everyone involved? Is there a solution to this conflict? What is it?

The third step in stopping the argument cycle is to observe the situation in as objective manner as you can. Look at the situation as a wise and objective third person. Imagine how a wise, balanced, and fair person would see the situation and what do you think they might suggest as a solution. This would be a good time to pray for wisdom to see how God looks at the situation.

Finally, dedicate yourself to finding a PEACEFUL resolution to the problem. This means that you are interested in finding a solution which will be good for everyone involved. Your approach should be one of a peacemaker, ambassador, or diplomat and not one of a warrior or soldier.

Once this has been processed in a careful and prayerful manner, then you are ready to engage the other person again in a healthy and positive attitude ready to find a mutually agreed upon solution. Express gratitude to the other person allowing you to have time to think about the issue. Assure them that your desire is to find a mutually agreeable solution to the problems.

Use the following advice from the Apostle James to guide you:

"Know this, my beloved brothers: let every person be quick to hear, slow to speak, slow to anger; for the anger of man does not produce the righteousness of God." (James 1:19-20 ESV)

Tell the other person you want to follow some simple guidelines. One that only one person will speak at a time and no one will interrupt the other person. Listening is not agreeing. It is simply listening.

Both people will limit what they say to three minutes. This can be done by using a standard egg timer. You can also find one on-line at http://www.online-stopwatch.com/eggtimer-countdown/full-screen/. The key here is to have a structured conversation in which both people can be sure they will be heard.

You then can explain that you have learned about a method of solving problems that may help in the conversation. Would they be willing to use it? If they say "yes" then explain the P.E.A.C.E. process with them. If they do not agree, then simply use it to frame your own thoughts and allow them to talk in any way they wish. So what is the P.E.A.C.E. process?

The P.E.A.C.E. process

The peace process seeks to have people define the problem that the relationship is facing, express their emotions about the problem, logically analyze the problem seeking all the possible sane answers to the issue, then carefully and prayerfully contemplate what the best answer would be to the problem, and then express that answer in a concrete and workable plan of action.

So the P.E.A.C.E. process is:

Problem defining

Emotions expressed

Analyze the problem logically

Contemplate a solution

Express this solution in concrete actions

How would this work?

- Problem - Each person will write out their understanding of the problem. Both will listen to how the other describes the problem. Attempt to come up with wording that works for both people on what the problem is and how it could be handled.

  - Example –
  - Person A: I think that the problem is that you are rude when we are talking about a problem.
  - Person B: I think that the problem is that you nag me about things
  - Combined problem: When Person B feels they are being nagged then they chose to respond in a rude way to Person A. How can this be improved?

- Emotions - Each person should list in writing their emotions when this occurs and share them with the other person.

  Fear, frustration, guilt, shame, optimism, pessimism, despair, hurt, sadness, ...Etc.

  For example: I feel put down when you are rude.
                   I feel like you are treating me like a child when you nag.

- Analyze - Each person should list every possible solution that they can think of to solve this problem.   This should be open ended brainstorming.
  - Example
    - Don't nag
    - Don't be rude
    - Develop a way to talk about a problem that does not feel like nagging.
    - Find a safe way to indicate that one feels that a remark is "rude"
    - Find ways to honor and love the person who is feeling treated rudely
    - Find ways to respect the person who feels nagged
    - Develop reminders to not nag
    - Develop reminders to not be rude
    - Read books on communication
    - Make a list of virtues that one sees in the other person and share that with them to reassure them that they are loved and respected
    - Give "nag" and "rude" poker chips to the other person when they fall into the destructive behavior.

- Contemplate- Each person looks at all the ideas that have been suggested and puts together what they feel would be a good strategy to solve the problem. Then they share their solution to the other person. Both listen to the other person's solutions. Note any similarities. Not any differences. Work to develop a Win/Win agreement that both people could follow. Pray with each other at this point and seek God's wisdom on how to find a solution

  - Example: We will meet once a week to focus on one problem at a time. I will not raise problems outside of this process. During this process we will not be rude to each other but speak and act in a respectful manner. We will pause if we think we are losing self control. You have the right to tell me if you think I am being rude or if nagging occurs.

- Express - Figure out a concrete plan to express this answer and apply it to the relationship. Do the solution that both agreed to try. Do this during the next week or month. Then plan to get back together and give each other feedback on how things are moving forward. Solutions can be improved upon and modified. Nothing has to stay in concrete.

Now this process will not feel as natural as having an argument. You may have to stop the process and take a breath again to keep things from getting elevated. One key is attempting to always paraphrase what the other person said after they make a statement. This makes sure that you really understand what is being said. It also gives them assurance that they are being heard. You can also ask the other person to paraphrase what you have said. Remember be focused on being a good listener.

The other key here is to be solution focused. If an agreement is reached in which you "win" and the other person feels they have "lost" then you can know that the solution will not last and you will be having this conflict again in the near future. If you decide to "lose" and let the other person "win" then this will lead to resentment and an expectation that they will let you "win" in the next conflict. These expectations are normally not met and so this lays the seeds for bitterness and lack of trust. Clearly a solution that did not satisfy either person is only harmful and not helpful.

Only a solution that is felt to be a "win" by both people will endure and help the relationship grow in intimacy. We need to focus on finding a real answer to the real problem. Now people can also admit they have not found a solution and then call upon consultants and counselors to help them find a solution. It is perfectly "OK" to know you don't have a good answer.

The final part of the relationship blueprint is craze. Now how can "craze" be part of a sane, stable, and spiritual relationship? Because sane relationships need to have passion in order to be stable and spiritual.

What is craze? – This is what we passionately care about. For married couples this is the place for romance and sexuality. It is also the place for "fun". This is also where people do things together that they both care about and enjoy.

This includes both those actions that reflect our purpose and our pleasures. People who share hobbies, exercise together, or feed the homeless together all bond. When we share what we are "crazy about" then we become emotionally intimate.

Some of us lose our playfulness as we get older. We forget that many times it is hanging out, relaxing, and having fun together that bonds us. Such times help us share laughter together and feel close.

As parents this is where we play and work with our children. Parents who create enjoyable moments with their children will have better relationships with their children than those who limit their role with their children to being "rule makers" and "rule enforcers." Now life needs rules, structure, guidelines, and consequences. However, it also needs spontaneity, freedom, creativity, and grace. Parenting is about finding the dynamic balance that combines these two into a energetic lifelong mentoring relationship with our children.

In friendships this is where we do fun things together or work together towards common goals. When friends stop spending time with each other then the relationship begins to falter. When we have less in common in what we do and care about, then we find that we just don't feel as close to each other.

Corporate cultures that place an emphasis on positive team work and creating an upbeat atmosphere that helps maintain morale understand that productivity and longevity depend on people having "fun" at their work place. People who are energized and excited get more done than people who feel under the oppression of a whip.

For married people this is where we need to put energy and time into dating on a weekly basis. One of the key elements of a successful marriage is that the couple continues to put energy and passion into dating each other.

Most people got married because they enjoyed dating. Most married couples stop any regular pattern of dating. The very activity that had made them feel like wanting to be get married they end. It really is not surprising that people feel they "fall out of love" after they get married. It is because they stop opening themselves to the "craze" that led them to get married in the first place.

To keep being "crazy" about each other we need to plan to date, have fun, and play together. It is by planning to have this as a regular part of our relationship will remain vibrant and alive with passion.

So we need to dedicate some time, energy, and focus on just having fun with the important people in our lives. This element is more important than we can imagine. People are attracted to what seems beautiful, encouraging, and enjoyable. Craze allows us to feel the joy of our relationships which sometimes fade when we get involved in conflicts.

So the blueprint to good relationships is clear. We must have commitment, communication, and craze. The health and vitality of any relationship can be defined by evaluating these three areas.

For those who would like to do some additional reading on these subjects let me recommend:

1. Plato, Not Prozac!: Applying Eternal Wisdom to Everyday Problems by Lou Marinoff

2. <u>Fun & Creative Dates for Married Couples: 52 Ways to Enjoy Life Together</u> by Howard Books

3. <u>Sacred Marriage: What If God Designed Marriage to Make Us Holy More Than to Make Us Happy</u> by Gary Thomas

Just like everything else that God created there is a structure to things that allows them to work effectively. When we respect this natural order of things we can work within it to produce better results. This is true of sane relationships as well. Follow the blueprint and you will find that your relationships will work better and last longer.

Reflective Questions.

1. List the ten most important relationships in your life. On a scale from 1-10 how committed are you to each relationship?

2. What keeps you from being a good listener? Why do other people not think you listen well? How could you improve as a listener?

3. How could you invest more time enjoying the people God has placed in your life? How could you increase the "fun" factor?

Chapter Five: Conclusion – The End of the Matter is Love

To have sane relationships we have to succeed at learning to love. Clearly, if we don't love well our relationships will not be healthy. Therefore, to understand love and how to increase our love for others is a vital aspect of having healthy human relationships. True spirituality can be summarized in learning to love God. All of our relationships are sane, stable, and spiritual to the degree that we have learned to love.

Jesus the Messiah teaches this the gospel of Matthew:

"One of them was an expert in the Jewish Law. So he tried to test Jesus by asking, (36) "Teacher, what is the most important commandment in the Law?" (37) Jesus answered: Love the Lord your God with all your heart, soul, and mind. (38) This is the first and most important commandment. (39) The second most important commandment is like this one. And it is, "Love others as much as you love yourself." (40) All the Law of Moses and the Books of the Prophets are based on these two commandments. "

(Jesus the Messiah; Matthew 22:35-40 CEV)

The 20th-century Rabbi Eliyahu Eliezer Dessler is frequently quoted as defining love from the Jewish point of view as "giving without expecting to take" (from his *Michtav me-Eliyahu*, Vol. 1).

In Christianity, the practical definition of love is best summarized by Dr. Thomas Aquinas, who defined love as "to will the good of another," or to desire for another to succeed. This is what it means for Christians to love others, including their enemies. Now we have to carefully define "good" and "succeed" here. But if we do that correctly then this concept is one that can help us learn to love others.

Dr. Thomas Aquinas goes on to explain, that Christian love is motivated by the need to see others succeed in life, and success in life is to be sane, stable, and spiritual people. Now how does this relate to our love of God? It is to love God so much that we want to see HIS will succeed on the earth in every aspect of reality. ("St. Thomas Aquinas, STh I-II, 26, 4,")

So love is critical to us succeeding in relationships. This leads us to a critical question.

What is love?

There are four Greek words that can help us understand love. The English word "love" does not really help us know the differences in the different types of love. But in the Greek languages there were many words for love which allows for some careful nuances to be made.

These four words are *Agape, Eros, Philo*, and *Storge*. By reflecting on these four words this can enable us to better understand the feelings of love we experience in our lives. Each of these words helps us to better understand the feelings of affection, compassion, loyalty, and passion we feel when we do love others.

Agápe (ἀγάπη *agápē*) means "love" and is used in many different contexts ranging from passionate love to an ideal love. In ancient Greek, it often refers to a deeper sense of "true love" or "committed love" rather than the attraction suggested by "*eros*". Ideally this love makes sacrifices for others due to an unconditional choice to care for and serve them. It is a very passionate love guided by very strong principles and energized by strong emotions.

The idea that *Agape* love is simply treating a person in the right way without caring about them emotionally is not supported by its use in the literature. It is a love that has been given to a person unconditionally but has within it strong feelings and commitments. We cannot satisfy our duty to show *Agape* love by merely acting right towards them but we must also feel right towards them. Agape would include the feelings of compassion, care, concern, pity, and honor.

Agape love becomes distorted when it enables addictions and destructive behavior. When it is twisted to mean that a person becomes a doormat and cannot say no. The danger in seeking agape love is that we begin to think that to love we must not think, judge, or discern. This is not true agape love but a misrepresentation of it. Sometimes love demands I say no. Love is loyal to the truth as well as

126

to the person. We must never sacrifice discernment for love, for true love is discerning.

Yet, to be able to give unconditional care, compassion, acceptance, warmth, and empathy to another person are vital expressions of love in our lives. We have to place people into our lives and love them not because of what they do or don't do, but simply because they exist. We have to choose to love them not their performance. This does reflect how God loved us in the Messiah Jesus.

Éros (ἔρως *érōs*) is passionate love, with sensual desire and longing. *Eros* however does not have to be sexual in nature. *Eros* can be interpreted as a love for someone whom you love more than just *a friend*. It is to love the beautiful in the person. All romantic love falls under this term. It is a feeling of attraction to another due to seeing in them a quality you admire.

I can show *eros* love towards people or things. I can love how a car runs and/or looks. I can love an athlete who performs well. I can love how my spouse looks on a particular day. This love is conditional. It is closer to our word "admiration".

The danger of *eros* is that it can be short lived and lack commitment. It is very fragile since beauty or effectiveness can be lost. It can become focused on taking emotional joy in what a person does or possess instead of who they are in their essence. It can look upon people as a "means" of attaining the feeling of love instead of being an "end" in themselves to be loved. The weakness of this love is that is conditional.

However, part of our life as human beings is to experience and know *"Eros"* love. We cannot help but admire something that is efficient, strong, or beautiful. God built us to admire such qualities because these are HIS qualities. It is just important that we know that this is not the most important or profound type of love. It is good to experience such love but not base our commitment to a relationship upon it. *"Eros"* love is the frosting on the cake but not the cake itself. It adds flavor to life but if it should fade or disappear, it must never lead us to be unfaithful to those whom we have a duty to be committed to and care about.

Philia (φιλία _philía_) This is the love of friendship. It is a dispassionate, stable, committed, and loyal love. It includes loyalty to friends, family, and community, and requires faithfulness, equality and familiarity. It can also reflect a common commitment to a common purpose or goal that unites the friends.

Philia is the stable love or our regular relationships. It is a bread and butter type of love. It is the feeling we have when we are part of a "team" that is bonded together to accomplish some common purpose. It is the loyalty we feel towards our team mates as we struggle to be successful. It is the feeling of "brotherhood" or "sisterhood" we feel with those with whom we have joined in a common cause.

Philia can become polluted when the common purpose we work on together becomes more important than our "friend" and so the person is lost to the purpose. It is distorted when loyalty to the "group" becomes the primary focus and value. "Friendship" then is used to manipulate people into unhealthy choices. This is what we mean by "peer pressure". This is one of the main dangers found in having _Philia_ type of love.

Storge (στοργή _storgē_) means "affection" in ancient and modern Greek. It is natural affection, like that felt by parents for offspring. Rarely used in ancient works, and then almost exclusively as a description of relationships within the family. Love or affection based on social duty and established relationships. It is the feeling that "blood is thicker than water".

Storge becomes distorted when we become unjust to others because of our affection for our family. When this emotion leads us to harm non-family members in the name of caring for family it has become misdirected. When _Storge_ leads us to betray another duty to another person for no other reason except the bond of blood then it is wrongly used.

Now each of these four types of love has a place in our life. We may love a person in all four ways. These types of love do not cancel each other out but can complement and strengthen each other. A sane person will strive to have all of these various types of love active in their relationships but clearly defined and balanced. Thinking about relationships without thinking about love is just not sane. Ultimately our relationships will be sane, stable, and spiritual to the degree that they are filled with love.

I would recommend that you read and use my book <u>Learning to Love in 27 Days</u> as a way to deepen your ability to love others in your life. This workbook will help you to deepen your vision of love and practice it in your daily life.

Conclusion

To gain from this book you need to now review it and make a list of every idea that struck you as you were reading. Develop a plan for using every truth that strongly impacted you. Don't lose what you have learned. Review and apply! This is the key to changing our behavior based on what we have learned.

May the Lord bless you with sane, stable, and spiritual relationships in your life.

Reflective Question

Rate these loves in your life right now. How important is this type of love to you? On a scale from 1-10, rate the significance of this love in your life.

Agape – Unconditional and serving love

Eros – Passionate love

Philia – Friendship

Storge – Family

Made in the USA
Charleston, SC
03 November 2015